BLOOM
WHERE YOU ARE

An Inspirational Journey of Failures, Victories, and Strength

JERRY L BLANK

PAGE PUBLISHING, INC.
New York, NY

First originally published by Page Publishing, Inc. 2019

ISBN 978-1-64462-412-8 (Paperback)
ISBN 978-1-64462-413-5 (Digital)

Printed in the United States of America

I lovingly dedicate this book to my wife, Denise. I honestly don't know where I would be without you in my life. You are the best part of me and keep me grounded. You are such an inspiration and a support system for me. Thank you for your unwavering love. I love you.

I would like to especially dedicate this book in loving memory of my niece, Lori Modglin Bishop. Her sense of humor and love for life were so inspirational to those who were blessed to have known her and witness her infectious laugh. She passed away at a young age, but her spirit lives on vibrantly in her daughter, Kaylee, who shares the same humor and love for life, caring for others and showing compassion at such a young age. Kaylee, your mother would be so proud.

Also, I encouragingly dedicate this book to my nephew, Tony Waller. Though the years may have sent you down a path that none of us could have foreseen, I have faith that you will continue to live your life for the purpose that God has intended. You are still loved and not forgotten.

ACKNOWLEDGMENTS

None of this would have been possible without God. I thank the Lord for my life of failures, victories, and strengths to use as an example through this book. I know He would not give me anything that I cannot handle.

I thank my siblings, Linda, Bill, George, and Fred, who have banded together, helping one another survive our rough past, and who continue to be a support system by piecing together stories of our family history for the purposes of this book. Thank you for helping to fill in the blanks.

My wife, Denise, has been my rock and my muse, helping me remember the stories and recording them. My son, Jason, has helped tremendously in typing and organizing my sporadic thoughts into coherent paragraphs. My two daughters, Michelle and Dawn, and their husbands, Jesse and Adam, have supported and encouraged me throughout this whole process. Likewise, my grandchildren, Jackson, Hunter, Sam, and Hannah, have kept me laughing by being the crowning jewels of my life and continuing to inspire me! Thank you. I love you!

Thank you to my extended family, family-in-law, and nieces and nephews who have all shown nothing but support, reassurance, and love as I bounced ideas and concepts off you all.

I'd like to express a specific appreciation to Karen Waller Stewart and AniKatrina Brianna for their comprehensive counsel and literary assistance. Additionally, I'd like to thank Charles Fineberg, Andrew B. Sanders, and John S. Sanders for their guidance and encouragement to pursue the creation of this book.

Special Thanks

Thank you to my dad, Robert Blank, Billie Blank, and Lila. We may not have had the most perfect family, but we were still a family, and you are still my parents. I have found that I must forgive you to allow myself to move on with my happiness and leave the past in the past. I can only hope that you found your peace and that you can see how blessed your kids are today from how we all bloomed where we were and to how we continue to bloom in life despite the struggles of our past.

PREFACE

People ask me why I decided to write a book. I simply say, "Well, I read one once." *Ha!* Honestly, though, I wanted to write a book to inspire people who think they don't matter, who think they are all alone, and who have been told that they are no good and that they will never be anything or amount to anything. Thanks to my son, Jason, and my wife, Denise, we were all three able to collaborate in helping to make sense of my handwriting, typing, organizing, and the phrasing of my thoughts into this book. The creation of this book comes from love and compassion to, hopefully, inspire people who are uninspired going through the motions of life because they are afraid of failure. If you feed the good, good will come forth; but if you feed the bad, then the bad will come to be! It's all about perspective and finding the joy in life to keep you positive and happy. We don't have to choose to be a victim. We all have a choice even though it may not always seem like it. Find your passion in life and be the best you that you can be!

INTRODUCTION

I don't think I am anything special, but if I can make it through this life, anyone can! I don't claim to be an expert. I am merely a person with sixty-five years of wisdom and experiences to share with the hope of helping others in need. Each facet of my life is an example of finding a sense of purpose and self-respect through humor, faith, and encouragement. The following is a collection of personal failures, victories, and strengths that have occurred through-out my sixty-five years of life.

This is my story.

CHAPTER ONE

I Was Born a Very Young Child. Ha!

Growing up within a traditionally strong German heritage, I was taught that family is always important. I can remember aunts and uncles, great-aunts and great-uncles, but I don't remember my own grandparents except for one—my father's mother, Frieda, whom he told us that while he was growing up, she used to clean for their neighbors and friends to bring in money since his father left her with four boys to fend for themselves during the depression. My father, Robert, being the eldest, delivered groceries for the neighborhood store owned by his uncle Frank to help his mother. Later Dad worked his way up and became a meat cutter at this same store.

I remember the day my grandmother Frieda passed away. I was with my father that day, and we went to her house. He sat me in a big chair in the living room, went into her bedroom, and closed the door. After a short time, he came out crying, picked me up in his arms, and said, "Mom's gone to be in heaven." This was the only time I ever remember seeing my father cry.

I guess the depression era was just a different time because there wasn't much joking around, and you just didn't tell jokes or laugh in a German household; but for some reason, jokes and laughter were very much alive with me. My wife, Denise, tells me that I used joking around and laughter to hide the hurting and pain in my life as I was growing up, and it carried over into my adulthood. As you read further, you will notice that there is nothing special about me. I have just been blessed with a passion for life and a compassion for others, family, friends, and anyone God brings in my life's path.

Alcohol was a problem with my birth mother and my father, Lila and Robert. Being German, it was custom to drink quite a bit. My mother, Lila, was much younger than my father. My dad just got home from the Air Force in World War II when he met my mother, and they married. As a decorated World War II Vet, he was able to get one of the houses the government built for the GIs. Lila and Robert started a family. Dad became the owner of a theatre supply company that provided concessions and theatre equipment to the surrounding theatres and other companies in the area.

Back in this era, almost every town had a movie theatre or a drive-in theater, creating a boost in business for dad. As the business grew, Dad had to travel a lot, leaving Lila at home with four children: Linda, William (Bill), George, and me. At this time, Mom began to drink while my older siblings were at school, and I was at home with her. I've been told stories by Linda, the oldest of my siblings, about how Lila would leave me in a closet for hours while she drank, or leave me in the closet so she could go out to drink. Linda said she would come home from school and find me in the closet with wet, dirty diapers and sometimes crying.

That was probably the same time that I looked up to my sister as a mother figure. I don't know if I really remember any of this part of my life or if I just chose not to remember. My father and mother divorced when I was about four years old. While our parents went through the divorce, Linda, Bill, and George were all sent to Alabama to live and go to school for a year with Lila's family. Since I was so young, my father decided to keep me with him, and to this day, I'm not exactly sure why he made that decision to be a single father while still working.

Bill, Me, our birth mother, Lila, George, and Linda

My father, Robert Blank: World War II Air Force

Later my father married Jewel (Billie), my stepmother; however, I never thought of her as my stepmother, but just my mom since she was there instead of Lila. She was nice and gave me special treatment through my early life. I had a secret friend who sent me cards and small gifts through the mail at different times of the year as well as for my birthday sometimes. Once I was sent seashells from Florida, and I remember getting two seahorses that Mom and I put in a fishbowl! I found out later in my teen years that all this time, my secret friend was my new mother, Billie! I think because I was the youngest of my siblings, that was the reason for the special treatment at the time until I was about five years old when my stepbrother, Fred, was born. I never thought of Fred as a stepbrother, but only as a brother, just like my other two brothers.

Fred, Dad, Me, Billie, George, Bill, and Linda

I don't remember birthdays or special events in our family, but the holidays were good. Some Christmases I remember were sometimes disappointing. One Christmas I got my brother's hand-me-down bike and two pairs of his blue jeans.

I really don't remember much until fifth grade, but I was held back to repeat second grade. I had problems in school, which were mostly my own fault, but I loved school even though I was not very good at it. If they had special education back then, I'm sure I would have been valedictorian. *Ha!* Education is the key to success and happiness, so staying in school is much more than just an after-school special.

Growing up, I was a bit of a loner and somewhat kept to myself. I was aware of my family issues and didn't want to cause any more problems by telling others about our family "secret," much less have friends sleep over for fear that my parents would get drunk, misbehave, and embarrass me. There were times where Dad drank and then beat me with a belt buckle and even physically abused Mom. I remember some nights when the two of them got so drunk they would curse and yell at each other. Dad dragged Billie down the hallway by her hair, throwing her into a cold shower, yelling at her to sober up. I sometimes cracked my door to see what was going on but then retreated back to my bed, hiding under the covers, hoping that I wouldn't be next. I was just so scared I prayed that my dad would just go away.

In some cases, I wouldn't even change my clothes in gym class just to hide the bruises caused by my dad. Seeing Dad like this was so scary and confusing as a child. I was always afraid of my father, and I just tried to stay out his way without giving him any more reasons to get upset. No child should ever fear their own father! I did have two good buddies whom I played sports with: one was an African American, and the other was an Italian American. Now, you have to understand that the era was 1969, where racism, especially in the American South in Memphis was *very* alive.

One day my two friends waited in the living room at my house while I changed clothes. My dad said hello to them as he passed and proceeded to tell me loudly back in my bedroom, "Get them out of my house!" We all left without question and went to my African

American friend's house. My Italian friend and I waited in the living room this time while our friend changed, and his dad walked through, saw us, and told his son, "Get them out of my house now!" So we left again. I guess it was just a different time back then, and we didn't try to go to our Italian friend's house. We were tired of getting thrown out of every neighborhood in the city of Memphis.

Sports was something I found that I was pretty good at. I played sports most of my life: football, where I was considered to be too small; basketball, where I was considered too short; but I was fast, so I ran track. Baseball was my passion, and it came naturally to me even though I had to learn how to catch the ball with a right-handed glove because Dad refused to buy me a left-handed one.

Me, George, Billie (Mom), Linda, Bill, and Fred

I finally got a left-handed glove from my church coach.

CHAPTER TWO

In My Family Tree, I Must Be a Bloomin' Idiot! Ha!

I believe that family is very important. Sometimes you must make the best of what you have. Children don't get to choose their parents. In our current times, with high rates of divorce, drugs, abuse, etc., children are often an afterthought. But listen to me, young people! You have the choice to go wherever and become whatever and whomever you desire to be. The relationship between you and God is the most important family you can have, and if you are aware with an open mind and open heart, you will see the angels that he sends to you throughout your life to help you overcome whatever problems life brings.

My father worked hard and provided for us by keeping us together when he could have simply sent us all away and not try to salvage our family after divorcing our birth mother, Lila. I admired him greatly, but I knew I could never live up to his expectations of what he thought I should become. It was almost as if he was annoyed with us just being kids. My brothers and I especially were not the easiest of kids to raise. There are just so many stories of our antics as kids growing up that seem to have made fatherhood even more difficult than usual for our dad.

There was a summer when my friends and I decided to try to break records. We thought of the brilliant idea to ride our bikes as far and as long as we could. We mapped it out on where to go and how to get there. We ended up about twenty-one miles away from our neighborhood and were too tired and cramped by that point to return home on our bikes, so I called my father to come to pick us up since he had a van, but he said, "You got there. Get back."

Luckily, one of my friends' dad had a work van and was able to take us home. Another record was trying to see how many soft drinks we could drink in just one day. The idea was thanks to a local store advertisement, so naturally, I accepted the challenge. I drank twenty-one bottles within eight hours. We never knew if that was a record breaker or not, but I was sick for about two days. Another record was a fast-food eating contest from the restaurant that I worked at on the weekends. The challenge was to see how many burgers you could eat in an eight-hour sitting. If you left the table for any reason at all, you were disqualified. One of my friends was small in stature, but he could eat like a horse and never gain a pound. This particular friend ate nineteen burgers within the allotted time, winning the competition only to find out that the prize was a punch card for ten free burgers. My friend simply responded "yay" unenthusiastically.

If us kids wanted some money, we had to earn it ourselves. All my brothers and myself ran paper routes, sacked groceries, and cut grass, along with other odd jobs that we could find. Although being kids, we did try to make the jobs entertaining and fun for ourselves.

As each of us grew older, the same paper route was inherited by the next brother, keeping the same route in the family for about ten to twelve years. When I took over the route from George, I had about sixty to seventy houses to serve. There was also a new apartment complex built that boosted my paper route up to three hundred customers!

Mowing lawns was a task since our first lawn mower was an old-school push lawn mower. George and I were finished mowing our neighbors' lawn, and George had the genius idea to flip the mower upside down and ride on it as I pushed him home. We were going down a hill as the mower increased with speed to where I couldn't keep up, so I let go. All I can remember was seeing the handle flopping in every direction as George tried to gain stability by grabbing onto the metal bar connecting the wheels. The blades were exposed since the mower was upside down and ended up cutting off his right trigger finger.

I followed behind, picking up the severed finger as we both ran home. Dad met us at the back door after hearing George screaming and seeing his bloody hand. I presented the finger to George. I guess you could say that I was able to give my brother the finger even though it was his own. Dad tried to stop the bleeding as he took George to the doctor. They tried to sew the finger back on, but they couldn't. Years later, we all have a good laugh about his stub. George even embraces it with many tricks by making it look like his whole finger is stuck up his nose or that he's doing a magic illusion of separating his finger from the joint, which still amazes our young grandkids today. Classic!

One summer on a Saturday, I was playing with our next-door neighbor's grandkids who were a few years older. We all went into their backyard even though my father told me I wasn't allowed. They had a small domestic farm with two chickens and a huge pile of hay. I remember it being so hot that day I saw one of the chickens lay a hard-boiled egg. We all climbed upon a pile of concrete blocks to throw rocks into the ditch that separated my dad's yard from theirs.

Like boys do, we began to roughhouse while six feet high on top of the blocks, and one of the older boys pushed me off, causing me to land on a pitchfork that was lying on the hay. The prongs of the pitchfork pierced my left leg just above the knee. When I looked down to see a hole ripped in my jeans, all I could think about was that my dad was going to kill me for ruining my jeans. The pitchfork fell out as I stood up. I limped home, where my dad met me at the back door and saw how much I was bleeding and then picked me up, cleared the kitchen table, laid me on the table, and pulled off my bloody jeans. My mom almost passed out from the sight of the gaping hole in my leg as she tried to stop the bleeding while Dad called Dr. Anderson, who lived just down the street. Since it was a Saturday, Dr. Anderson told us to meet him at his office about five minutes away.

The doctor examined my leg and said, "This is your lucky day. If it were about a quarter of an inch deeper, you might not have been able to walk again."

He stitched me up, and Dad took me home. I now understood why I wasn't allowed in the neighbor's backyard and never went back.

Showing off my pitchfork wound in the backyard, 1961

I believe that our family tends to have a streak of bad luck, as most people would call it. Another hot summer, George and I were mowing our neighbor's lawn down the street. This neighbor's front lawn was a huge hill, and George was the genius who thought to tie a rope on to the handle of the lawn mower, letting gravity work for us and then pulling it back up to move it over and let it down again. As we pulled it back up, the rope loosened, causing the mower to speed down the hill and into the street. At the same time, our father drove down the street to check on us and ended up running over his own lawn mower. We spent the rest of that summer paying our father back for the lawn mower.

I think that our antics and creativity came from our father. Dad was tough, and I think sometimes uncaring or unjust, but I believe he loved us in his own way. My father was a great dad many times, but other times we never knew what version of our father we were going to get. One of the "great dad" moments that I cherish is when Dad made a jeep for us kids to drive around. This jeep was way ahead of its time, preceding the typical electric, kiddy vehicles found in almost every toy department today. This jeep had one push button to start it and no brakes or doors.

I remember being so excited and loving that car so much that I drove it everywhere, even to places that were off-limits. Dad told me not to go too far, to stay close to the house, and stay out of the street. Of course, being the daredevil kid that I was, I decided to push the boundaries and go all the way down the street. As I went down the street, passing its incline, I started gaining momentum going faster and faster downhill toward the crossroad.

Struggling to maintain control, I wasn't sure how to slow down since the jeep had *no brakes*! Seriously, why did Dad not put brakes in that thin? I held on tight and turned the steering wheel, causing me to crash into a white concrete pillar with the street names stenciled on. The impact was so hard that I knocked the pillar over out of the ground. Of course, my dad found out and met me at the corner of our street, checking out the damage. I don't remember if he was concerned about my safety, but I do remember him inspecting the jeep to find out that the collision only put a small scratch on the bumper. Even though he had to pay the city of Memphis to replace the street pillar, he laughed with pride at his handiwork in making such a sturdy, tanklike jeep. Glimpses of my dad smiling and laughing are moments that I choose to remember him by.

One day I was just sitting in the jeep when a man walked up and asked how much it would cost to buy it. I informed him that it wasn't working after a flood shorted out the electrical wiring. The man didn't care and said that he could fix it. I went to ask my dad how much we could sell the jeep for, and he quoted the man one hundred dollars, which back in that day was a significant amount of money, especially to a kid. Of course, Dad kept it all and didn't attempt to give me a couple of bucks even though I was technically the salesman.

The jeep Dad made for us. Bill driving and me
poking my head up from behind him

When we were not busy trying to make our own money, my brothers and I played ball in the backyard. One time my older brother, Bill, pitched, and I was at bat. He threw it hard to where I couldn't hit it, but finally, I got a piece of it. The ball sored crashing through the window of our next-door neighbor's house. George was in the outfield and ran to retrieve the ball and decided to throw the ball back into our yard, breaking another window from inside. Dad's response was, "I can understand busting one window going in, but throwing it back breaking another window going out? That is what stupid is."

My siblings were always important to me as a young boy, and they continue to be important to me as I still admire and respect them to this day for who they have become and everything that we all have endured together. Whether we were aware of it at the time or not, we all helped and supported each other when dealing with our father's, mother's, and stepmother's drinking problems. To this day, comparing stories and individual experiences with my brothers and sister, we still uncover new information about what exactly happened to our family. I saw and still see my sister as more of a mother to me than our own two mothers, especially Lila, who really suffered from alcoholism, losing self-control.

I was told that when I was three, Lila threw me into a closet, locking me in while she tried to burn the house down. Thank God Linda was in the right place at the right time to call the fire department and Dad in time to stop this tragedy from happening. I was also informed that this happened twice before Dad made the decision to send Lila away to receive medical and mental help, eventually ending with their divorce. Linda remembers hearing Dad say, "I have to protect Jerry."

Recently learning this information now at the age of sixty-five upsets me to tears thinking about what might have been, but I am so thankful for my sister and brothers for keeping me alive through my early years when I was so defenseless. They were the beginning of my army of angels that God placed in my life. My oldest brother, Bill, was always so smart, bestowing motivation and advice, whether it was asked for or not. I watched and learned from him in everything he did. At times, he was much like a father to me, filling the void when Dad wasn't able to be the father I needed him to be.

In later years, Bill told me that he was surprised at how much I could remember from our past as I did because I was so young back then. Bill was the "college man" and also the one who taught me how to drive, even though I tore up the clutch in his little, white Corolla. George was very much an inspiration who taught me how to be my own person and stand up for myself. Also, he and I were partners in crime on several occasions, coming up with brilliant ideas to get in trouble. My younger brother, Fred, impressed me with his intelligence, much like our brother, Bill.

My siblings and I were fortunate enough to have extended family members supporting us during the hard times with our parents. Among the aunts, uncles, and cousins, I specifically am thankful for my second cousin, Paul Koehler, who was always around, not only as a cousin, but also as a true friend while I was young. In Paul I found a great support system with undying encouragement in my life and my interests. Even today when we randomly bump into each other, he still is as genuinely supportive and caring as ever to hear what has been going on in my life and with my family.

I spent most of my childhood trying to make my father proud and happy with me. I tried to make him notice me and accept me for who I am and not for what he wanted me to become. However, I guess I never did really reach that acceptance with my dad. In my later teen years, I learned that I couldn't force someone to be happy and like me for who I am in order to feel loved. I realized that I had to be happy for myself and love and accept myself with all my imperfections so I could move forward and grow into my greatest potential to live and enjoy life for me and for those I love.

At some point in all our lives, each of my siblings and I moved forward with our own lives and left the stressful and emotional pressures of our family behind. My sister, Linda, found her escape by getting married even though our father was against it. Bill went to college defying our father's wishes to work for the family business after a short life as a boxer. My second-oldest brother, George, was a bit rebellious, according to our father's standards, and they argued about our father's drinking problem.

One iconic moment I remember spurring George's escape is when Dad was drunk and started kicking over George's motorcycle, ripping chords out, causing George to retaliate by busting the windows out of Dad's van. This is an example of many that made me look up to George as an inspiration in my life to stand up for myself and my beliefs. I left to pursue a baseball career. As the youngest brother, Fred stayed until he graduated high school. He was always very business-minded and ended up taking over the family theater supply business, which is now running three generations strong. As time went on, Fred and I became fellow athletes in many sports, bringing us closer as brothers.

I believe we are put here to help one another despite our differences. We may not have control over our environments, but we do have control over how we react and endure to survive until we have the power to change our environments. So many kids past and present secretly live the same childhood as my siblings and I and are forced to grow up too quickly to deal with the adult issues of abuse, alcoholism, and other serious topics. So if you're a teacher, a mentor, a volunteer, or even a family member, don't hesitate to reach out and encourage, support, and possibly take action, and *love* those kids whom you know are living a rough life. Anyone, anything, any word, and any moment can have a positive or negative impact on your life and others around you.

CHAPTER THREE

Seventh Grade Was the Best Three Years of My Life. Ha!

I remember in fifth grade at Cherokee Elementary in Memphis, my teacher, Mrs. Platt, was one of the most encouraging people in my life who knew of my love for baseball and that I maintained sports stats from the professionals to my school team. She used my interest in these stats as an example to show me how math is important and gave me a newfound respect for math in everyday life and improving my grades. I also became a history buff because of her. She knew I loved Babe Ruth, so she bought a book about him for me. I'm sure I read it about fifty times, and I even did book reports based on it, and I still have that special book in my office today. So my reading, history, and social studies grades all improved. She would always say that she wanted my autograph before I made it to the major leagues.

One day at recess, I hit a ball that broke through her classroom window.

We went to get the ball from her, and all she said was, "Jerry Blank! Did you hit that ball?"

I said, "Yes, ma'am," and she replied, "Great hit!"

I never forgot her over the years because that was the point in my life where I started thinking about how treating people and what you say to people really matters. Because Mrs. Platt was such a special teacher to me, as a positive influence in my life, I learned that I had the power to choose to be either positive or negative no matter the situation. No matter what the situation is or how big or small, I try to do everything with passion and compassion.

Baseball has always been the constant factor in my life. I remember playing Little League when I was about ten years old. My three coaches were Mr. Carter, Dr. Score, and Mr. Dehardy. These three men were honest, good, and loyal men who inspired me at such a young age. They made sure that we learned the game but also that we had fun and enjoyed the game as well. My team was undefeated, and I personally had high stats of hitting ten home runs for the season. I was also the star left-handed pitcher because back in my time, we didn't have coaches pitching for us at that age level. We just played ball!

At about twelve or thirteen years old, I played for our Trinity Lutheran Church team. There was one game where I was the pitcher, and my father and stepmother finally came to see me play. Our church pastor, Reverend Paul Martens, had to extensively encourage them to go because until that point, my father never made any effort to watch me play. The park was packed! I pitched a good game of six-inning strikeouts with twelve walks and three hits, but no runs. I hit two home runs and then was walked with the bases loaded, and we won with the score 11–0! My teammates and I were so proud and excited about our hard work! When I got in the back seat of the car, I waited a few minutes and finally got up the nerve to ask my father what he thought about the game.

He said, "Why didn't you strike out that black guy?"

All I could do was cry. This was just one of the many things my father said to me over the years that made me realize at an early age that there was never anything I could do to be good enough for my dad and live up to his expectations.

Mr. Carter on the left and the Trinity Lutheran Church Team Champs!

In junior high, I was in desperate need of guidance since my father was progressively getting worse with his drinking problem. At Sherwood Junior High School, I was blessed to have a positive role model, Coach Ayers, who saw athletic potential in me as a baseball player and invited the high school coach, Coach Cordell, to show off my skills and see me in action as a left-handed pitcher. That same day, the two coaches were shocked to see a little middle schooler hit a ball into the street across the entire outfield. Coach Ayers was a big believer in running, and he made us athletes run, sometimes forgetting about us until we ran what felt like ten thousand miles. If anything, I was at least in the best shape of my life. He invited me to his church, which was the first time I was in a different church from my own. The visit exposed me to a new perspective of worship where people were laughing and telling jokes that was way different from the strict Lutheran upbringing I was used to.

High school was interesting. While I was dealing with being a teenager and continuing to endure hardships at home, the world was dealing with the Vietnam War, the rise of the hippie movement, and the civil rights movement. I continued to find solace in sports and friendships. Having my reputation proceed me from my junior high years, I made the varsity baseball team as a freshman.

The upperclassman players helped me out like older brothers, however, they were still keen on carrying out my freshman initiation. They were notorious for making underclassmen jump in or push them into a mud pit. When it was my turn, I straddled the pit and took off running, but I decided to give in and just let it happen. Ticked off, they chased me, caught me, and personally dragged me through the mud pit not once, but twice, exacting their revenge for me being a difficult underclassman. I guess it was what I deserved for ticking off the entire baseball team. Of course, I made quite the reputation for myself as a trickster in high school, bonding with most of the school athletes. There was a time where a guy was lifting the girls' skirts in the hallways as some fellow jocks tried to stop him. I was at my locker when I heard my friends yell at me to stop him. All I did was simply open my locker door, making the guy run right into the metal locker door, falling flat-out cold.

My friends gasped, "Jeez, Jerry! We asked you to stop him, not kill him!"

Coach Cordell had a background of playing professional ball for the St. Louis Cardinals, and he was strict; and although I feared him, I looked up to him. I admired him since we both were small in stature and left-handed. I saw that if he could make it, then I could too. I learned more about baseball from him than I ever did in my entire athletic life. Coach Cordell loved my hustle and had high hopes for me as I grew stronger and faster, progressing as an athlete.

In my junior year of high school, he even paid a visit to my dad, telling him that I had a special athletic talent with baseball. He continued to say that I had a chance to go college on a baseball scholarship. Naturally, my dad said, "No. Jerry needs to stop playing games. He should be worrying about getting a job after high school." At that point, Coach Cordell realized what I was dealing with at home, and he told me that he would help me to the best of his abilities as a coach without overstepping parental boundaries.

If anything, I learned the value of having a hard-work ethic from my father. Learning how to manage my time, to balance all my responsibilities at a young age, I went to school; immediately after that I ran and maintained my paper route, then went back to school for baseball practice, and then went home to do my homework. If you have a passion that you cannot stop thinking about, it is worth pursuing and making sacrifices to keep it.

One time during ball practice, I kept throwing curveballs and striking out one of my teammates whose weakness was curveballs, and Coach Cordell stepped in to bat, telling me to throw him a curveball. I did, but it did not curve and ended up hitting him hard.

The whole team simultaneously gasped with "Oh crap!"

He approached me at the pitcher's mound and said, "When I tell you to throw a freaking curveball, you throw a *f*@king* curveball!"

He went back to bat, and I threw him a curveball again, and then he smacked it far into right field, hitting the roof of the gymnasium while boasting, "Now *that* is how you hit a *f*@king* curveball!"

"Force" is the word for Jerry Blank as he readies for championship play against Kingsbury.　　　　　Tuesday, May 27, 1969

During my high school days playing on the baseball team, I received an invitation to attend a two-day baseball try out for the Cincinnati Reds in Jackson, Tennessee. I asked my father to drive me, but he refused. Bill learned of this and offered to drive me. When Bill and I drove up, I saw there were junior college players: some very good players, and older players all there for the same thing. Feeling intimidated, I told Bill not to worry about reserving a hotel room because I felt I wasn't going to be passed through the tryouts; however, I made it through the first cut, causing Bill to scramble around to find a room. I was a left-handed pitcher and an outfielder, even though I wasn't very strong as an outfielder. The other players could hit home runs, run like deer, stand six feet, four inches, and weigh 250 pounds; and then there was me at five feet, five inches, and a 140 pounds with a desire, love, and respect for the game. It was very much a David-versus-Goliath moment. However, a scout named Chet Montgomery saw a desire, love, and respect for the game within me.

My first time up to bat, I got a hit, stole second base, and scored on a single-base hit. Next, I was grouped with the pitchers, but I knew that I was special since everyone needed a left-handed pitcher. During one inning of a game, I pitched a strikeout and two ground balls. I didn't have a strong fastball, but I did have a lot of junk, which is a baseball term for different pitches such as changeups, off-speed, etc. I knew that if I kept the ball down, I would be successful.

On that Sunday, I made it through the cut to play summer ball in Florida with two other players. Celebrating and feeling proud, I called my father to share the news, expecting the long-awaited praise, but he simply replied, "If that's what you want," and hung up on me. From there, I quit school and earned my GED, left home to travel to Florida, and play ball all over the state. One very special moment that I will forever cherish is when I was called up to play a game joining the starting lineup of the Cincinnati Reds in spring training! I remember walking out to center field, taking in the entire stadium filled with cheering fans and turning to see baseball legends and Hall of Fame players all around me and feeling so humbled to have even been sharing the field with them. About a year later, I got a knee injury that ended my baseball career, so I came home, but it will always be a great and life-changing experience to remember.

Even though my father greeted me with open arms when I moved back, he said, "I told you that you wouldn't make it.," reminding me that I will never be able to please him. I moved out and got a job to support myself. Also around this time of my life, the lottery for the military draft came about during the height of the Vietnam War, where young men had to wait for their number to come up and go into action. Four of my friends joined; one of which was number 6. Three friends never came back, but one returned and was never the same. My number was 341, allowing me to go to college.

College was great! My father and I were not on speaking terms, and I continued to play baseball on a small, competitive team for Hannibal-Lagrange College. Hannibal is a small town in Missouri and is considered to be "Mark Twain" country.

Looking back now, I see how God placed people into my life to continue to inspire and lead me forward to my life's purpose. I will never forget my Psychology professor, Dr. Mansky, who could annihilate anyone in ping-pong and was one of the most Christian men I have ever met. He was similar to the absent-minded professor always showing up late for class, but in his teachings, he taught me how to relate the Bible to everyday life for inspiration. His lectures were somewhat hard to follow, with the randomly inserted joke here and there, getting himself sidetracked. I remember he once told me that he had to award me a "weak B" on a test, to which I said, "We need to work that B out and make it a strong muscular B!" *Ha!*

Dr. Mansky was a missionary in Ethiopia, and he shared several stories from his time there while randomly walking into the classroom not knowing if anyone was there or not. A piece of his wisdom that has always stuck with me to this day is, "You might not agree with me, and I may not agree with you, but both growth and understanding come from respecting our differences."

Another professor who made a lasting impression on me was my History professor, Mr. Freeman, although he would call himself a "History Expert," which he was. He was known to be rather passionate and strict with his lessons even though he did actively protest during the hippie movement in his college years. His teaching was rather unorthodox, dividing the class into sections to have each one study the revolutionary war from different perspectives, such as Paul Revere, England, and the colonies. This task helped broaden my thinking and begin applying this outlook on life, trying to understand other people's perspectives, different life experiences, and hardships.

Mr. Freeman also taught Government, where he sometimes revealed that he was not the biggest fan of the American government, saying that it should get out of the way of the people with its excessive regulations, laws, and red tape. He was a wealth of knowledge, and he was not afraid of asking questions for a deeper understanding. I remember him saying, "I love my country. It's the government that scares me. America is still the greatest country in the world. Why do you think everyone is trying to live here?"

The greatest words I remember him saying are, "It doesn't matter if you're Republican or Democrat, old or young, male or female, religious or not, or different in races. We can all learn from each other to help the greater good. Education begins with listening and sharing ideas that are different from our own to gain a broader perspective. It is up to us to find common ground. Any change is up to you."

Mr. Freeman knew that I loved to tell jokes, and on occasion, he asked me if I had any jokes about history or government to share. Naturally, I would oblige. One oldie but goody joke that I shared was, "Mr. Freeman, you are so old that when you went to school, there wasn't any history. It was current events." He went outside the classroom to regain composure, leaving the class to their laughter and their admiration of my nerve to even joke about him since he was so stoic and serious as a teacher.

Of all my teachers, Dr. Kenneth Moore was by far the best professor that I have ever had in my entire life. He was an extremely educated Bible scholar who spoke six languages and taught the Old Testament and the New Testament, along with Greek, Hebrew, and Latin. He was a very thin and pale-skinned man in his sixties who always slicked back his hair, wore a black suit with a black tie, and black-rimmed glasses. The students joked that he could lie down in a coffin, and he'd be ready to go. Six languages or not, he always spoke in a calm, monotone voice. I remember his first words to the class was that he also taught pig Latin on the side. This phrase made me laugh out loud and informed me that Dr. Moore had a sense of humor.

I remember he asked me one time if I spoke any other languages. I replied, "I know a little Greek. He runs a pizza parlor in New York." The class didn't know how to respond and waited to see what Dr. Moore would say. I could tell he was laughing even though he tried hiding it by crossing his arms and covering his mouth with his hand.

Dr. Moore's classes were very difficult yet very informative. One time he wrote on the chalkboard in Hebrew while lecturing in English and Greek. I looked around the room to see my classmates just as confused as I was. I decided to stand up at my desk until Dr. Moore noticed and stared at me all while continuing his lecture.

He paused, took off his glasses, and held them with crossed arms, asking, "Mr. Blank, do we have a problem?"

I replied, "Yes, sir, I'm having a hard time taking notes. Everything thing you are teaching is going over my head, so I thought that if I stood up, it would all hit me."

Of course, the class erupted into huge laughter, breaking the tension. This was the first time I ever heard Dr. Moore laugh out loud as he dismissed class.

Another time, Dr. Moore was in a good mood, expressing what a beautiful day it was as he opened the classroom window, set his books on the window ledge, and looked out from the third floor. He continued to ask the class what we were going to do with this beautiful day and said that we had the choice to do whatever we wanted. He suggested that we could make it a good day or a great day while gesturing as he knocked his own books out of the third-story window. Obviously, I died laughing on the floor.

Dr. Moore asked, "Mr. Blank, do you think that's funny?"

I said, "No, sir. It's hilarious!"

Dr. Moore replied, "Then you wouldn't mind going to get my books."

I did as he suggested, but I laughed the entire way. My classmates even said they could hear me the entire trip.

As I returned still dying of laughter, Dr. Moore uttered the words "Class dismissed."

When I graduated from Hannibal-Lagrange College with my associates in arts degree, Dr. Moore approached me and said, "Thank you for making me laugh."

Like my sense of humor moving Dr. Moore, I can only hope that this book entertains and helps others who are lost and in need of encouragement and laughter.

Chapter Four

Have You Found Jesus? I Didn't Know He Was Missing! Ha!

College was a great time of my life helping me grow as a person and as a Christian. As I mentioned, I grew up in a traditional German household heavily influenced with Christian values. Now, I understand that religion may not be the answer for everyone. At some point, though, we all need something to believe in to give us hope. For me, believing in God and having faith has given me hope and helped me survive some of the toughest and darkest moments in my life. People have questioned my faith, stating that if God was loving and caring, he should not have allowed those evil things to happen; however, I see those moments as lessons to grow stronger and wiser to help in the future or to mentor others who may be suffering.

I remember learning from several men of God as I progressed through my life. Each one had a special influence at that time of my life. My first pastor was Reverend Paul Martens at Trinity Lutheran Church in Memphis. Pastor Martens used to be a missionary in China for years before joining my family's church. Through the years he got to know me and my family, and I'm pretty sure he was aware of what was really going on in our house. He had a way of talking with my father that made my father respect him. As I mentioned before, Pastor Martens was able to perform the miracle of coaxing my father to see me play one ball game. Thanks to Pastor Martens, I was set up for a lifetime of hope, faith, and love through my relationship with God.

Pastor Martens and me on my confirmation day

Aside from my rough upbringing, there have been moments throughout my life that have not only influenced me, but also taught me lessons to shape my views and strengthen my faith. A moment that I will never forget was when I was around fifteen or sixteen. I was at a picnic with several friends. People were spread out eating at tables and on the lawn visiting, while others were swimming, jumping and swinging on vines into a lake. There were about thirty of us boys and girls just all enjoying the beautiful Saturday weather. Among our fun, a couple of Christians showed up to witness to us about Jesus and getting saved. One girl was very annoyed and told them, "I have the rest of my life to be saved and accept Jesus. I'm young, and I just want to live my life how I want to!" She then walked off with others to go swing into the lake. No more than a couple of minutes afterward, several people screamed and yelled in horror. The girl had swung into shallow water and landed on rocks, breaking her neck. Once the paramedics came onto the scene, they reported that she died instantly. My friends and I were all shaken with immense devastation. Her last words have haunted me my whole life. None of us really know just how much time we have in this world. We *must* enjoy life and take advantage of every moment given!

At the age of twenty-one, I was saved by Jesus and felt the call to pursue ministry. I was able to speak at several youth rallies and church functions, where I met Jonny Bell, who later became a roommate and lifelong friend. Jonny and I teamed up to do student-run church services where I preached and he sang. After many youth-led services, our leader informed us that several other churches requested Jonny and me to visit. God was blessing us.

One story in particular was forty years in the making. As a "new Christian," you are stimulated with high-energy inspiration to fix the world and save everyone. I and about nine others decided to witness to a group of bikers who had a cookout party with strippers in the parking lot of an adult gentlemen's club. Motorcycles were all lined up, the beer flowed, barely clothed girls danced, and the music blared. We showed up with small Gideon Bibles to hand out to everyone. To our surprise, some people listened to us and, of course, some brushed us off. There was one biker guy that I had made eye contact with who looked pretty tough with his hair in a ponytail, sunglasses, a wallet chained to his pocket, an earring, and a black leather biker vest.

As I walked up to him, he put his sunglasses on top of his head and said, "Don't waste your time, boy!"

With my little Gideon Bible in hand, I said, "It's never a waste of time to talk about Jesus."

I handed him the Bible and told him that I previously wrote down some inspiring passages on the inside cover for him to read later.

He took the Bible and threw it up on top of the club's roof. I just looked at him with confusion and a little bit of fear as he said, "Now, what are you going to do about that?"

I reached in my back pocket and presented him with another little Gideon Bible that was green. I told him to read it later when he was alone. He then took it and placed it inside a bag on his bike, and I and my team left the club feeling proud that we did some good!

Fast-forward to forty years later, I'm umpiring a coach-pitch game in a small town outside of Memphis. A young man that I umpired for several years approached me and shook my hand, informing me that I was about to umpire his son's first coach-pitch game. Afterward, the same young man invited me to the stands, telling me that someone said they knew me.

As I made it to the bleachers, there was an older man in a wheelchair with a gray ponytail, one leg missing, thick glasses, and a black leather biker vest that said "Bikers for Jesus." I shook the man's hand as he asked me if I remembered him. I told him I didn't. He pulled out a little green Gideon Bible and said that I gave him that Bible forty years ago! The Bible looked old and worn, with the page corners bent and torn, and the cover barely showed signs of faded green.

He said, "I kept this one since I threw the first one you gave me on the roof of a club that day."

As tears filled my eyes, I felt so overwhelmed. He continued to tell me that it took him a while to understand, but he accepted Jesus twenty years ago. He showed me the passages that I wrote inside the cover and told me that he read those passages over and over again until his pastor explained it to him.

The man said, "I can't believe that our paths crossed again. I've been waiting and wanting to say thank you."

We both hugged, and I told him I thought he was going to kill me those many years ago.

He said, "I thought about it. Just kidding."

I could not believe how God used me as an immature teen to influence the life of a hard-core biker guy! I don't know if you believe in angels or not, but I do. I have always felt the loving hand of God in my life. As I matured through life, I became very aware of people (angels) that God sent my way. I've also become aware of the way God uses me in other people's lives. My faith keeps me humble and more receptive to the meaning of my life.

About three years after that reunion at the ball field, the young man and I met at another ball game where he told me that his father passed away. He told me that his dad preached to several of his biker buddies and grandkids from that little green Bible. A change for the better begins with you to positively impact others as I have been able to do. Hope, encouragement, and love can spring from anyone, anywhere, and at any time. Just remember, what we choose to do with our lives makes a difference.

Witnessing and preaching was all great, but I just didn't have "the call" to formally become a man of God. As the saying goes, many are called to serve, but few are chosen. I knew God had a plan for me, and people told me that I had "the gift" for preaching, but I just didn't feel that special connection to do God's work as my passion. I wasn't too sure what I was meant to do with my life or where to go. According to some, there are many people from the Bible and in today's life who may not be considered to be proper candidates for God's message, but he loves everyone. Everybody has the potential to be the moral fiber that we desperately need in this world.

Later in my years, another influential pastor was Pastor Weise, who was also a pillar of hope and support in dealing with my family issues. He and Pastor Martens both officiated my wedding and became an important part of mine and my family's lives. I remember a special moment and lesson from him where I prayed to make it through to another day, to be the best husband and father I can be, but I kept falling asleep in the middle of praying. So I asked Pastor Weise if he thought God was mad at me, and he replied, "What better way to go to sleep than in the Father's arms!"

My kids learned so much of how a Christian should act from the many church camps and retreats that he helped chaperone. He also officiated all three of my kids' confirmations as they grew into young Christian adults. Unfortunately, as the kids grew into their teen years, the traditional way of the Lutheran church was missing specific emphasis to help our teens continue to grow. Our family began to seek and visit other churches to see what would fit best.

My sister and her daughter, Lori, were active with Bellevue Baptist Church and invited my family to join a service or two. I knew of the church from umpiring and refereeing ball games where I got to know several members of the congregation. We gave it a try and felt at home with the pastor who was so influential and passionate about the word of God, the late Dr. Adrian Rogers. After a couple of visits to the congregational services and individual classes, my family and I decided to join as members. One special Sunday night, Dr. Rogers said, "We need to get our baptism on the right side of salvation!" as he baptized my whole family together.

Dr. Adrian Rogers was one of the greatest men of God that I had the privilege of knowing and learning from.

Eventually, life obligations took over, and my family and I failed to attend church as much as we should have. The kids became adults and moved out, living their own lives, and Denise and I found a church close to our home. Dr. Sam Brassell became our new pastor. He reminds me of the talent that Dr. Mansky had of making the Bible come to life and relatable in today's life, mixed with the preaching abilities of Dr. Rogers and the comforting compassion of Pastors Marten and Weise.

Someone asked me, "Have you seen the movie, *The Bible?*"

I replied, "No. I read the book!"

I am blessed to have found the ability to use my life for spreading love and laughter as a ministry for others. I now know that I was trying to impress the wrong father, when my heavenly Father was there all along, loving, accepting, and guiding me through life. I don't believe that life happens by chance. Each of us has a purpose. If God can save me and use me, he can save and use anyone. If you live life with an open heart and open mind, you can change yourself first and then find peace, direction, and a sense of purpose for your life. A question that helps me is, "If you were arrested for doing good deeds and spreading laughter and love, would there be enough evidence and witnesses to convict you?"

CHAPTER FIVE

Turns Out, the Better Half of Me Is Female! Ha!

After college, I came back home and attended my family's church with my parents, where at least someone in my family has been a church member for over a hundred years. There I met the most beautiful girl that God ever created, whose grandparents also attended as members. She sat beside me in Sunday school where I learned that her name is Denise Waller. Almost immediately I called her uncle to get her phone number, which he obliged. However, he called her first to warn her about my future phone call. We went to youth functions together, and we talked for a while. One memory in particular was during a youth coed touch football event. Even though I had my knee brace on from my baseball injury, I went out for a pass from my brother. As I caught the ball, Denise ran up to tackle me, but my knee brace locked up, causing us to collide and fall to the ground. She had grass stains all over her pants. All I could say was, "I have some explaining to do to your father. I guess you could say that I literally swept you off your feet!" Now that I think about it, I don't know why I didn't just let her tackle me. That was June 1977.

As Denise and I dated, I was twenty-four, and she was twenty. We both worked, but did not make much, so we were creative in figuring out what to do and where to go on our dates. We frequented arts-and-craft fairs, flea markets, the zoo, museums, recreational parks, and other events and locations. One park in particular became our favorite romance spot with luscious gardens, trees providing shade, several walking trails, and a romantic red bridge overlooking a fish pond and the occasional ducklings to feed. Denise and I, along with most other people, typically visited the gardens on Sundays after church.

There was a time I just knew that I wanted to live the rest of my life with Denise, so I began to shop for a ring and planned my proposal. When it comes to asking someone to marry you, it can be very nerve-racking, but special. Some people go all out with an airplane flying overhead, followed by a banner asking the question, and others will take the opportunity at a sports event to ask the question on a jumbo screen. These examples are all good ideas, but by asking such an important and personal question in public, it places a lot of social pressure on the other person, and there is a risk of the answer being "no."

One specific Sunday in October 1977, Denise and I slowly took our time strolling through the gardens. It was a beautiful day with a beautiful lady. What more could a young man want? We sat down on one of the many benches that lined the trails, and we talked for a while as I internally battled nerves and struggled to muster up the courage to propose. Hoping she wouldn't notice, I avoided eye contact, looking around to find my bravery. I remember spotting the number plate on the back of the wooden bench we both sat on. It was number 21. My eyes finally met Denise's, where I found comfort in her gaze.

I said, "I don't know if you have noticed, but I'm getting very serious about you. I don't have much to give or offer you, but..." At this point, I knelt to one knee, shaking and clearing my throat, continuing, "One thing that I can promise you is all of my love, my heart, and even my very soul to you for the rest of my life. Whatever we do and wherever we go, we will go through it all together." I took her hand and slid a modest but significant ring onto her finger as I asked her to marry me. We both began crying as I continued to say, "Don't answer me right away. Take your time to think about it, talk to your parents, and when you're ready with an answer, let me know."

A week later, I picked her up for a movie date. As I drove us to the theater, she randomly brought up the topic of the proposal, saying, "About your question, the answer is yes." I was so caught off guard that I ran a red light. I pulled over in a store's parking lot, where we hugged and kissed, thus, starting the whole planning process for the wedding while balancing the upcoming holidays.

We were married December 31, 1977, at 4:00 p.m. That's right, New Year's Eve. I told my soon-to-be father-in-law that he spent the whole year providing for Denise, but I get to claim her on my taxes. *Ha!* We were married in the church where we first met that was built in a very historically traditional, gothic style. I know it seemed so sudden, but when you know, you just know! Fast-forward to thirty years later for our thirtieth wedding anniversary when I went back to our favorite garden, planning to take a picture of "our bench" where it all started. To my surprise, I saw that the bench was gone!

The park was going through renovations, which included replacing the wooden benches. I asked some of the construction workers if they knew where the old benches were, and they led me up a hill to a huge storage building where I saw several benches stacked all over each other. Overwhelmed at this sight, I began to share the proposal story, explaining why I was there to the maintenance supervisor. He told the workers to break down the pile of benches to help search for bench number 21. Before long, I spotted the bench off to the side by itself. I couldn't help but believe that this was meant to be. The bench looked a little worn from the years, but so did I. I asked the supervisor how I would go about purchasing the bench and who could help me. After finding out where I parked, he told his two men to load the bench onto the back of my truck and told me the bench was mine for free because they were going to destroy them anyway.

He said, "That's a great story. Take the bench home and make your wife happy."

I went home and gave the best thirtieth-anniversary gift to my wife, sharing the story with our children, family, and friends. The bench now sits on our patio in our backyard. Not too bad for an old romantic!

Finding the right partner in life is a blessing. My wife says that marriage is great with the right person; she just hopes she finds the right one. *Ha!* Honestly, though, I thank God that he included Denise in my life to be my best friend, the mother of my children, my lover, and the love of my life. We have had forty years and counting of loving, laughing, crying, and getting through trials and tribulations, supporting and leaning on each other.

With Denise, I found a different perspective of what a family is, especially the roles of a mother, a father, and grandparents. The Waller family thrived and continues to thrive on the family values of hard work, putting family first, and compassion. Denise's family was a breath of fresh air in contrast to my city life and a broken home. She and the Wallers accepted me with loving and open arms, and I was able to build close relationships through my humor, especially with Denise's mother, Marion. For some reason or other, I was always able to make her laugh. Marion was the most comforting person who was always so calm and seemed to always have a plan. I think it came from her cake decorating, always solving unforeseen problems through creative thinking.

I've always admired Denise's father, Kenneth. He was one of the smartest men I have ever met in my life with his common sense, handgun, integrity, and his love for his family. He taught me how to be an honorable hardworking man, a loving husband, and a supportive father and grandfather. He also taught me how to be a moving target by giving me a shirt with a bullseye on the back, but I never wore it at his house. Denise's sister, Karen, became like a second mother to our kids, always stepping in to babysit, allowing Denise and I to go out for a date night. Nowadays she still continues to be a huge part of our family's life, and she has gotten pretty quick with her humor, fighting back at my little jokes and putting me in my place. I believe that God brought not only Denise into my life, but also the Waller family, providing a loving and safe environment.

Life with Denise has been and still is blissful; however, most of our problems have been minor and usually based on finances. We may not have much, but together we have creatively survived life in true MacGyver style. I can't fix or repair anything, but that's why God gave me my good ole country-girl wife! She grew up on a farm in Arkansas, where she learned how to fix almost everything if it broke. Her family made it work through creative problem-solving. Denise told me many stories of how she, her mother, father, four brothers, and her sister all worked together to tend to their crops, mend their clothing, and make life work on the farm. The city boy that I am, I learned how to break things at an early age. I'm the master of destruction, and Denise is the master of construction! Even now, if something needs to be fixed with our house, for example, I would want to hire a professional, but my wife would say no. More than likely, Denise and her sister, Karen, would instead put their brains together and come up with a solution, roll up their sleeves, and begin to fix whatever the problem is. I soon learned to just let them go and stay out of their way.

Denise and me, December 31, 1977, at Trinity Lutheran Church

Young people and couples always ask Denise and me what our secret is to a long and happy marriage. I tell the guys to keep quiet and do what she says. But honestly, we have found that making plans for long-term goals are great to map out where you both are going in life together. Short-term goals are also helpful with achieving small victories along the way to pursuing your long-term goals. Make sure you both are on the same page constantly, checking in with each other to make sure you both are still wanting the same things from each other and from life as a couple and not as two individuals.

Before getting married, you *must* talk about *everything!* Put it all on the table with no secrets and no surprises. Talk about each one of your hopes and dreams, aspirations, politics, religion, wanting children or not, parents, upbringing, sex, interests, and anything else; but above all, do not go to bed mad at each other. Listening is very, very important for resolving any differences or misunderstandings! That is why God gave us two ears and one mouth. You must put the other before yourself. I've never really liked the saying "Behind every good man is a good woman." You both need to be equal, side by side, and look out for one another.

I had a good friend who dated a lady for two years and got married. After three years of marriage, they disagreed on children. She wanted kids, and he did not. After talking with him, he said that in the two years of them dating and talking about marriage, the subject of wanting children never came up. Now they are divorced and don't really know why. He excuses it as them growing apart. I told him that they were never together to begin with.

Some couples get married for all the wrong reasons. Some people merely tie the knot based on physical attraction, but looks fade; however, I'm blessed to have a wife who is still as beautiful as the day I met her. If you marry for money, just remember money runs out eventually. Money is insignificant compared to loving each other, and you both can work together to find a way to survive financial problems. You can always rely on God together. I believe a couple that prays together stays together no matter what.

Bedroom etiquette can also make or break a marriage. Sex is a wonderful thing, but you must talk to learn about each other's boundaries as you explore each other. Someone once asked me if I smoked after sex. I replied, "I don't know. I've never looked." *Ha!* Just remember that God brought you both together to become one physically, intellectually, emotionally, and spiritually.

Another factor of marriage to be aware of and discuss is the in-laws. Parents need to get out of their kids' way when trying to help. Life decisions must be made by the couple. It's okay for parents to support, love, help, and guide. You can give experienced advice, but *only* if requested.

When our daughters, Michelle, the oldest, and Dawn, the youngest, talked to us about getting married with their "chosen ones," they each told their significant others that he had to ask her parents (especially me) for permission to have her hand in marriage. Michelle's boyfriend, Jesse, first called me, but he didn't say anything and hung up.

He mustered up enough nerve to call back, and I decided to help him by asking, "Is this 'the call'?"

He sounded very intimidated on the phone and replied, "Yes."

So I continued to say, "We know our daughter loves you, and we do too. You have our blessing, but don't tell Michelle that I made it this easy for you."

Our youngest daughter, Dawn, dated her boyfriend since high school. Adam's asking for permission was a little different than Jesse's. He called us, asking if we were going to be home for a few minutes. He paid a visit to our house, sat us down at our kitchen table, and proceeded his "five-point presentation" of how he was going to take care of our daughter. He informed us of his financial savings and a ten-year plan for their life together, including children and how he and Dawn prayed about taking this big step into marriage.

I told Adam, "Welcome to the family, but you do know that I will be your father-in-law, right?"

Adam replied, "I know. We've prayed about that too."

Michelle and Jesse were married on the same date as Denise and I, letting Jesse claim her on his taxes after I spent the whole year providing for Michelle. This was definitely my karma for doing this same thing to Denise's father. It's not nearly as funny on this side of the joke. Then Dawn and Adam were married at the same time as us at 4:00 p.m. The girls both told Denise and I that they superstitiously chose the same time and the same date as us, saying that it worked out for us forty years. As a father, that thoughtful gesture showed respect, not only for Denise and me as their parents, but it also showed respect for the sanctity of marriage.

Each story of my two sons-in-law reminds me of my time when I asked Denise's father for her hand in marriage. Now, you must understand that I'm a city boy, and she is a country girl raised on a farm. I drove all the way to their house in the middle of rural Arkansas. My situation was similar to Adam's, but instead of just sitting down calmly in the kitchen, Denise's father joined with a pistol sitting on the table.

He proceeded to say, "I understand you have something to ask us?"

Staring at the gun, I replied, "Nope! I believe it can wait."

Both Denise's mom and dad laughed, and her father said, "Welcome to the family."

My wife is the greatest of all my angels that God blessed me with in my life! She saw right through my humor and accepted the hurting and scared man who was still trying to be accepted. She didn't try to change me, but instead she helped me heal and move forward with my life through love, support, and a lot of prayers. I tell her every day that she's the luckiest woman in the world, and after forty years, I almost have her convinced!

Chapter Six

Who's Your Daddy? Just Call Me King. Ha!

I love children! I was once a child myself, even though my grandchildren don't believe that I was ever as young as them. Children are such blessings of innocence and wonder, helping adults view the world through different perspectives as a parent, uncle or aunt, and grandparent.

Being a parent is a great blessing and an honor to have created a whole new human being that you are responsible for protecting, loving, and molding into a better human than your generation and those before you to, hopefully, continue spreading good in the world and passing it on to their kids, creating a legacy. But there isn't a handbook on the best ways to be a parent. Like life itself, you can take advice and learn all that you can to prepare, but in the end, you just learn as you go!

Every child is uniquely different. What may have worked with your parents on you, and your grandparents on them, may not necessarily work on the kids of today. As the old saying goes, "The times are a changing!" One thing that is universally certain, all kids *must* be provided for and be loved to feel special. Just remember who the parent is. Kids don't need a best friend who's lenient with rules. Children learn at an early age how to use parents against one another in order to get what they want. It's called manipulation—you know, what we adults do to each other on a daily basis! *Ha!* In contrast, they also don't need limiting discipline or a strict military drill sergeant, but rules should be set to teach and protect them on what they can and cannot do. There is a delicate balance to enjoy the relationship of parent to child but also maintain boundaries with authority.

One of my wife's friends parented her kids in a very relaxed way, letting them do whatever they wanted. She expressed her free-parenting as letting her kids explore to allow them to learn at their own pace and in their own way. She believed that the world was at her kids' disposal to do whatever they wanted. Whenever they visited, I politely policed her children by telling them, "No." The kids looked up at me with very confused and surprised looks. I then realized that they were told, much less heard the word, "no." It was a new word for their vocabulary.

One other visit, the kids played and ended up breaking something personal of mine, to which the mother excused it again as the kids exploring and finding their way. I heatedly replied, "Let them find their way back to your house and break your stuff." Offended, she and the kids left. They still came over to visit every once in a while, but while they were at our house, the children knew that they could not play with my stuff. It might have been a new and hard lesson for the kids to learn, but the boundaries were set. The world is not individually ours to take and to make our own. Some people are taught the selfish concept to always try to get something from the world, rather than learn what they can contribute to the world to help improve life. We share the world with several billions of others, and we must learn to respect other people and their properties. I believe we can all have and enjoy our freedoms, but not at the expense of others' freedoms and properties. Not only is this a vital lesson to teach kids, but some of us adults could use a reminder and be aware of this as well.

At this point, I want to take a moment to remind everyone that it takes two to start a family. The female is no more entitled to the kids than the male and vice versa. The both of you created the child together, and the both of you are equally as responsible for the child's wellbeing together. Now, I must address all the fathers. Some men think that they are fulfilling their part by getting their wife pregnant, maintaining a job to provide the necessities, and staying out of the way to let the wife raise the kids. You're wrong! You're barely doing the minimum to help! You need to get involved and help the mother out. She is as new to being a parent as you are. Let her take the lead with her maternal instincts, but you must be ready and waiting in the trenches, anticipating her directions. Guys are so afraid, or at least I was, to handle the baby for fear of breaking it, but you won't. Those little things are resilient!

Sometimes the dads feel like they have been neglected, and they don't feel as special in the eyes of their wives once the child arrives. This makes dads feel useless and unwanted, promoting the idea of not getting involved with childcare responsibilities. Although this may happen, I have found other ways to get involved and stay involved by helping to take care of the other responsibilities around the house. I did the grocery shopping, laundry, the cleaning, and anything else to help out. Most importantly, I strongly insisted that my wife take a break while I took over to tend to our kids. That's right, they are *our* kids!

You're both not only there to care for the kids, but you both must be there for each other too! She will need your emotional support with possible moments of feeling overwhelmed and potential effects of hormonal imbalances after the pregnancy. She might even be angry at you for no logical reason, but you just continue to love, help, and support her. Moms, you need to help the dads out too with love, *patience*, and understanding as the dads try to help, even though their way may not be exactly up to your standards. Be thankful for the fact that they are at least trying. Let them help, and don't try to take on all the responsibilities all by yourself. Just like a marriage, becoming a family requires an equal partnership. Remember, you both are still best friends, husband and wife, lovers, and now parents together. Give yourselves a date night to still keep the romance and time for each other aside from always tending to the kids. Having children is great, but don't lose yourselves in the process.

With my and Denise's siblings having children before us, we both got a glimpse of parenthood through our roles as an aunt and uncle. We were able to discover how each other would approach certain situations and deal with certain behaviors in learning how far our limits can be tested. Additionally, we were able to act as mentors to help our nieces and nephews if they needed us. One specific time that I cherish was when I was asked to help a nephew play in a father-son basketball game since his father couldn't make it. I was able to show off my athleticism, surprising everyone. Hopefully, I made my nephew proud. Scoring points or not, I was honored and happy that I was able to step in and keep him from missing the game. I think that Denise and I have been able to build relationships of trust with all my nieces and nephews. Through the years, they have come to us for advice or help no matter the situation, knowing that we would not judge them and do our best to help if possible. Just like parenting, being an involved aunt and uncle is an ongoing learning process. Even today, we still are able to provide wisdom and help for our nieces and nephews who may be struggling to find their life's purpose. I am so honored that they respect us enough to hear our advice.

Denise and I began trying to start our own family after two years of blissful marriage. We were blessed with our first of three children. Michelle was born, and I, of course, thought that she was the most beautiful and perfect child that God ever created, but the years would soon change all of that! *Ha!*

A lady at church saw me with Michelle in her carrier and told me that I was going to be a great dad.

I paused, looked at my beautiful wife, and then told the lady, "I have been trained by the best!"

I did, however, take the compliment and internally accepted it as a challenge, knowing that fatherhood was going to be an ongoing learning experience. The saying of "a mother's work is never done" also applies to the work of a father.

About two and a half years later when Michelle began walking and talking, my wife told me that she was pregnant again. This took me back a little. I was concerned about how I would love a second child as much as I did the first one. I wondered if I could have enough love to go around. God once again showed me the way by blessing us with our son, Jason.

When Jason was born, my nephew, Johnny, who was a great baseball player himself, said, "Great, another left-handed pitcher in the family!"

I replied, "Only if that's what he wants to do, and if not, then I will support him in whatever he does want to do!"

With two small kids, parenting didn't get any easier, but I wouldn't have had it any other way. Michelle was very happy to have a brother and had no trouble being an older sister, acting motherly and bossing him around! Jason loved playing with Michelle and learning by watching her. It was interesting to see the two of them getting along, but still being two completely different individuals.

Another two and a half years later, Denise informed me that she was pregnant yet again! I thought whatever we were doing every two and a half years, we needed to stop it! This time around I wasn't so worried about having enough love, but rather being able to properly provide for my family. Dawn was born, and we were very grateful after facing some complications with her birth. Denise and I decided that having three kids was enough. Besides, we were blessed with one of each. Not having a handbook or an instruction manual on parenting, Denise and I banded together as a team to raise our precious, little ones. We had a system of using notepads with written to-do lists of what needed to be done for the day and for the week. Denise made a list of what she needed me to take care of, and I did the same for her, even though somehow my list was longer. This was a great way for us to stay on the same page and keep communicating, while both of us were busy tending to the kids and working. This game plan worked for us and still continues to be successful to this day.

As the kids grew up, Denise and I allowed and encouraged them to explore different interests. Michelle was a Brownie and was a cheerleader for Jason's soccer team, and she discovered her love and passion for music. Jason found his interests with art and drawing. He particularly was interested in how cartoons were made, so I showed him how to make a flip-book, explaining that was how his favorite cartoons were able to move! Dawn became our little sports star athlete. She loved sports and being active in softball and soccer, and she was very talented in both. All three kids are very special, and I'm glad I was able to be an influential father in their lives.

Our family of five grew closer together as the years went on. I would still play softball with the church team as my family went to cheer me on! This was really special to me since my own parents barely made it to one game when I was a kid. The love and support I was denied as a kid, I found in my wife and three children. We never claimed to be the picture-perfect family, but Denise and I instilled in our children important values and morals of love, sharing, and compassion toward others, with an emphasis on communication and the importance of a relationship with God.

I personally made the conscious choice to be a better father than my own. My siblings and I decided for ourselves to end the alcoholism with our generation, for fear that it was hereditary. I was scared to discipline my kids, afraid of losing control like my father, unfortunately making Denise mostly be the "bad cop," while I assumed the role of the "good cop." All three kids had their differences and fought like normal siblings do, but for the most part, they got along well. All three of them participated in marching band during high school, with Michelle playing trumpet, Jason playing drums, and Dawn playing the clarinet. Denise and I are proud of each of them, as they all graduated from high school and college and entered the world as adults. Taking a note from my book, but not this book because it wasn't written yet, of course, they each chose a profession to help others and continue creating good in the world. Michelle went into law as a paralegal. Jason thanks me for teaching him how to be silly and laugh at himself, helping him pursue the arts as a theatre actor for youth and a freelance graphic designer. Dawn went into the health industry as a registered nurse.

Denise, Me, Jason, Dawn, Adam, Michelle, and Jesse, 2018

I can honestly say I am truly blessed with my family, but there was a time when I thought I might have lost it all! In 2011 on New Year's Eve day (mine and Denise's anniversary), I was serving papers when my chest began to hurt. It was difficult to take a deep breath, so I decided to drive myself to the hospital where Dawn worked as a nurse. I walked into the ER and told them that I believe I was having a heart attack. I tried to talk to Denise on the phone; but at that point, the staff went into overdrive, putting me in a wheelchair, taking me to the back where six people took my phone from me and pulled off my clothes, started an IV, and checked my blood pressure.

I asked one of the nurses if I did have a heart attack, and she said, "You are still having a heart attack right now!" Everyone talked over me and about me, saying *stat* this and *stat* that, like they do on the hospital TV dramas.

After the chaos ended and my vitals were stable, I told the nurses, "I haven't gotten undressed that fast since my honeymoon!" They, of course, laughed, and my little joke seemed to have calmed them all down from the rush. It was also therapeutic for me to find humor and make this stressful situation lighthearted. Then a surgeon came in to insert a stint to open up the main artery. It turned out that my surgeon and I knew each other from me umpiring him a few years back. I knew he was a golfer, so I told him that whenever I play golf, I take two pairs of pants in case I get a hole in one. The surgeon laughed and warned me to stop since he was inside my chest, trying to place the stint at that moment. Afterward the doctor said that everything was okay for now, but I needed to go through a double bypass surgery to avoid having another heart attack.

Two and a half months afterward, I went into surgery about a week before my birthday. Dawn exercised her networking skills in the hospital and put together an outstanding team of angels in the form of doctors and nurses who took great care of me! During her shifts, Dawn even stopped by to check on me while I stayed in the ICU. After several hours in surgery, Denise told me that the waiting room was filled with all my siblings and their families, my children, my nieces and nephews, friends, church members, and my always loyal cousin, Paul Koehler.

Once I was fully recovered, I was back to normal and better than ever, and I had time to think about all the people who prayed for me. I was so overwhelmed with love and support, feeling so blessed to have had that many people show up just for me! It was a wonderful feeling of love and acceptance that I had been searching for in parts of my life with my dad, baseball coaches, work, and myself.

To this day, our family grows closer together than ever with each new life experience, whether good or bad. Denise and I occasionally take a moment to sit back in awe of how she and I created this wonderful, loving family. We constantly talk about our kids with pride and joy in seeing them continue to grow as caring and productive adults with their career achievements and career changes. They each share my sense of humor and compassion, pursuing careers to further help people on a more personal level.

Michelle said that she is thankful for me teaching her the life lesson of how to love others with compassion, as she is now pursuing a teaching career. Jason is striving to become a registered dietician. Dawn told me that she is thankful for me teaching her the value of hard work and how it pays off, as she earned her master's degree and became a nurse practitioner working in neuroscience. Both of the girls' husbands have become more like my own sons, firing jokes back at me even though they have yet to reach the high-level caliber of my humor. *Ha!* Jesse is the IT computer guy currently working to become a high school Physics teacher, and Adam has a talent in graphic design and works in law enforcement. Denise and I gush with pride to see our family continue to grow as our own kids and sons-in-law become parents and aunts and uncles. My wife says the only child who never grew up and left the house was me.

I may refuse to grow up, but my sense of humor and ability to still play and act like a kid at heart allows me to connect with children of all ages, including my own grandchildren! Having grandchildren makes me feel like my life has come full circle. When our daughters began talking about having children, they asked Denise and me what we wanted to be called. We ran through the list of possible names: Grandpa and Grandma, Grandfather and Grandmother, but I simply said that I wanted to be called "King"! Of course, that didn't go over too well. Eventually, we settled on the names, Nana and Papa. Reflecting back on my life, it is amazing how my resume of titles continues to grow from Jerry to Husband to Uncle to Dad, and now Papa. With each new title comes a new chapter of life, new adventures to experience, and new stories to tell, and I love every minute!

Jackson is our first grandchild by our oldest daughter, Michelle, and her husband, Jesse. Jackson is a super talented, young kid who is now eight years old. I believe one of the main lessons I have helped Jackson learn is how to have confidence in himself and not to be afraid of trying new experiences in life. He explored sports and found an interest in baseball, just like his Papa, naturally. As soon as I discovered he was left-handed like me, I took it upon myself to immediately buy him his first left-handed glove so he wouldn't have to struggle like I did at his age. He also has a love of art and a curiosity of how things work and are put together, which he shares with his dad, uncle Jason, Nana, and even his great nana (Denise's mother, Marion).

Our second grandchild, Hunter, is the firstborn of our youngest daughter, Dawn, and her husband, Adam. Hunter has such a peaceful demeanor and a caring personality. I hurt my hand once, and he kept asking me if I was okay and even made his parents call to check up on me. I can see that he gets his bedside manner from his nurse mother, Dawn. I believe I taught him that it is okay to be silly and make people laugh. Once he realized the power that the gift of laughter is, he loves being silly just like his papa! He is also talented in sports, especially baseball. This kid can hit! He shares a love of drawing like his dad, Adam, and uncle Jason and loves the outdoors. He is super smart in figuring out how to play video games at only five and a half years old, following in his dad's footsteps.

Jackson's five-year-old brother, Sam, is our youngest grandson and is what we call, a live wire. My wife insists that he is undoubtedly a mini version of me. Sam is our little daredevil, climbing up and jumping off anything and everything without a care in the world. He loves life! Since Sam is a mini-me, I try to help him learn the hard lessons that I still struggle with: stop, listen, and think before doing. Just like me having an interest in most different aspects of life, this kid bounces around from loving superheroes one day to an interest in dinosaurs the next and even wanting to be a garbage man. With all three of our grandsons, their growth has been in part due to Nana's boot camp, where their parents get a break, and Nana teaches them life lessons.

Hunter's two-and-a-half-year-old sister, Hannah, is our youngest grandchild and our only granddaughter. Our very own miss independent roams and runs all over the place. Her own mother nicknamed her, "Hurricane Hannah." She has a sweet little smile and knows how to use it to have and keep all of us wrapped around her little finger. She has a great little laugh. I can honestly say that I made her laugh out loud for her very first time when she was just an infant. It was a very special and funny moment luckily caught on video.

All our grandchildren still have both sets of their grandparents, which is something I didn't have. All their grandparents are actively involved in birthdays, cookouts, holidays, ball games, and other events. I feel so blessed and loved that my own family today is the result of my faith and strength that have directed me through my past struggles.

A family is the key to happiness in life, whether it is your birth family, your own family created with your spouse, or people that you select to be your family as your greatest supporters. Loved ones will always be in your corner, rooting you on. They see your potential to be the greatest you that you can be even though you may not see it. Be careful what you pray for, you just might get it. Of course, from the beginning with Denise, my father was against it and said our marriage would never last, but forty (and counting) years later with three children, two sons-in-law, and four grandchildren, here we are!

Sam, Hunter, Papa, Hannah, and Jackson, 2018

Chapter Seven

I Heard the Call, But It Was a Wrong Number. Ha

I believe that we all share the same goal of striving for a happy life by pursuing our passions. We all may be living at different stages in life with different experiences, but this common goal of happiness is greater than our differences no matter what stage of life we are in. I have worked many jobs and professions looking to fulfill God's plan for my life. Through each occupation, I have learned new things from people from all walks of life, influencing my personal and spiritual growth. Each connection provides an opportunity for me return the favor by empowering and inspiring others.

The one common aspect of all my past jobs has been my natural talent for sales. I believe that my talent extends from the many jobs I had as a kid—learning how to package products and phrase selling points to sound enticing to customers. One particular incident from my childhood was when my dad brought home a case of product called the "Pic" that was essentially just mosquito-repellent burners. The product came in a small box with a little tin stand and two coils that you would burn like incense to place around the patio, picnic tables, or anywhere you wish to keep mosquitos away. My dad and I tested it out, discovering that the product actually worked; so he asked me to sell them for fifty cents each, along with my paper route. With a smug grin, Dad continued to say that one case contained a gross, assuming that I didn't know what that meant.

I quickly shut him up by responding, "Okay. So I have to sell 144!"

This was at the beginning of the summer, and I told him to order five cases. Reluctantly Dad said that if he ordered them, he couldn't send them back. I assured him I could sell them all, and I even made a fun bet out of how many I could actually sell. Dad placed the order. Being the selling genius that I am, I taped two boxes together and priced them for one dollar each, selling them twice as fast to my paper-route customers, surrounding neighborhoods, and to fellow church members. Sales went so well I even had repeat orders, causing us to not only sell all five cases, but my dad had to order two more just to fulfill the rest of the lingering orders! It was a surprisingly profitable side business for that summer, but Dad kept all the proceeds to pay for all the things that I broke and tore up. As I reflect back on this memory now, I can't help but wonder if this was Dad's plan all along to trick me into paying for the damages I caused throughout my childhood. I didn't even know he was keeping score!

In everything I do and experience in my life, I meet some of the most interesting people and develop lasting relationships through my jobs. I worked for a dishwashing company, selling chemical products and cleaners to restaurants and other businesses in need of dishwashing solutions and services. This was not the safest job that I've had, with several close calls of company trucks breaking down, losing a wheel, or teetering over the edge of a deep ditch, along with transporting and transferring hazardous chemicals that could burn your eyes and skin. However, I was able to make connections with almost every client that I sold to and maintained business with. The mutual respect that I give others and my personable attitude made selling easy for me to be real and get to know my customers on a personable level. You can't sell a product you don't believe in. Because of these relationships, I was awarded salesman of the year out of the entire nation with record-high sells.

I also worked in sales for a bread company, where I cracked jokes, making business owners and managers laugh by saying, "Selling bread was a great job because I got to loaf around and make lots of dough!" After a while, I was dubbed by many as the "Crummy

Bread Man." Again, thanks to my personable relationships with the clients, I was also able to maintain record-high sales and was awarded salesman of the year out of the whole country.

Another profession that matched my God-given talent for sales was a "tote the note" used-car lot. It was a great business providing hardworking people, who may not have the best credit, to drive off in a car with just a down payment and legal identification. The owners of the lot were very good Christian people. The business began with the owner buying ten cars and working to sell them until he sold nine of them, driving the tenth car home. He continued this process by increasing his inventory each time until his business was born.

After a few years, he brought the family into the business to help wherever they could. They all developed a credible reputation in the automobile business industry. I personally bought a few cars from them over the years from one of the sons-in-law of the family that I knew from umpiring baseball. From our business-to-customer relationships through the years, I finally ended up working for the company.

Naturally, I sold many cars over the eight years I worked there, helping the business to grow and flourish. A running joke emerged, stating that I sold a car to a blind man twice! Seriously, I did! The man was a retired mechanic who could see, but not well enough to drive. He bought cars for his friends and family members to use with the condition that they would drive him around to do his daily errands. Here's a man who is paying it forward by helping his friends and family in need of cars, and I was able to be his angel to help him make it happen. Through the years I developed and maintained a friendship with my boss. I enjoyed working for a company and alongside an honest Christian boss helping people get back on their feet, providing affordable and dependable cars.

CHAPTER EIGHT

I Call 'Em Like I See 'Em Even Though I'm Blind. Ha!

As you know by now, sports, especially baseball, has always been an important part of my life. I believe sports and athletics help build character, leadership, and teamwork. Of my various professions, umpiring and refereeing ball games have been a major part of my life, which I continue to do to this day. Before my life was changed by the semi-pro tryouts, Ms. Z gave me a summer job, when I was about fifteen or sixteen, umpiring youth baseball for the city of Memphis. Umpiring helped me gain a different perspective on baseball, and I think it made me a better player. I have also refereed basketball, football, and lacrosse. I explained to my wife that umpiring and refereeing not only satisfies my passion for sports and the game, but it also helps me to bring home extra income. My wife helped me realize that umpiring and refereeing sports is also my own form of ministry, by God using me as an angel to reach people in need or just connect with others.

I have made lifelong friends with other sports officials: Chris B., Todd E., Mark T., and Keith R., all of whom I've umpired about a thousand or more games with. In my fifty years (and counting) as a sports official, I have witnessed so many generations of athletes come through the Memphis area playing basketball, football, and baseball who have gone on to play in college and sometimes even become professional athletes. I also have met so many families and their kids who grew up and came back to tell me that I made a positive impact on them through the years. My favorite games to referee and umpire are the youth games. They are so fun! One thing that has been consistent through all my years as an official is that parents are crazy, strict, and at times ridiculously embarrassing when it comes to their children playing sports. Some parents try to relive their childhood, and some try to live the athletic life that they never had through their own kids.

Others get too caught up with the idea that sports are teaching and learning tools for extracurricular credit to get their kids into college. Then others believe that their child is the greatest ballplayer God ever created, even though that kid couldn't catch a cold if they tried. *Ha!* Mostly a number of parents go too far and see their kids as a cash cow, if they are good enough, to become a pro athlete making a high-dollar salary to support them. They forget it is just a game! Let the kids be kids. Let them learn how to play the game and how to respect the game. Not everyone will become a pro athlete, but sports can continue to be a beacon of happiness and joy throughout life as it has been for me. I use my time to empower the kids and to calm the parents.

An example of this reminds me of a time when I umpired a youth tournament in the Memphis area, where a coach asked my opinion about his son's athletic skills and his potential to continue playing after high school. I said, "He is only eight years old! Let him learn the game and enjoy it. You shouldn't put pressure on him or yourself. You should use this time to strengthen your bond together as father and son. There's nothing more important than the bond between a father and son." Even though I couldn't change my past relationship with my father and sports, I wanted to advise the dad and remind him of the precious time he has with his son before he grows up and leaves home. I can only wish that I could've bonded with my father over sports as this young man has with his son.

It seems that just like I learned from my elementary teacher, Mrs. Platt, you never know just how much of an impact you may have on a person just by the way you talk to them and treat them. To this day I still have people approach me and thank me for making them laugh or instilling some wisdom that made a positive change in their lives. These people shared something that I may have said to them and explained how it stuck with them throughout their lives. I recently learned that I have now umpired three generations of one family. A lady told me that she showed sports photos of her three children to some family members and friends at Christmas, and she realized that I was in almost all those photos. Her kids even played different sports, but still I happened to be in those photos as an official. She told me, "Jerry, I have more pictures of you than I do of my own kids!"

Another time when I umpired a tournament, a young, five-year-old boy was up to bat and just kept missing the tee. His proud momma just couldn't understand why her Little Leaguer could not hit the ball off the tee. Fast-forward to the third game, where I decided to move the tee as low as it could possibly go. The young boy came up to bat and gave a swing with all his might. He finally hit the ball! He was so happy and confused as to what to do next and looked at me with a puzzled face.

I yelled, "Run!"

Immediately he took off running to second base and then all around the field as the other Little Leaguers followed, chasing him all around. Everyone in the stands and on the field just stopped in their tracks, laughing hysterically at the whole ordeal.

I told his mom, "I'm sorry. I told him to run, but I didn't tell him which way!"

These stories keep me laughing throughout my life and remind me of how all the different people I have met impacted and continue to impact my life.

Because I am a big kid myself, I love youth sports for the unpredictable and fun moments. You never know what those kids will say and do! I was umpiring a game where it was the teams' first live pitch instead of tee ball. After the game's last out, a little freckled-face catcher dressed in all his catcher gear and, mask in hand, jumped up and down with excitement and began to head toward his team's dugout, but then ran back to me and asked, "Did we win?"

I was honored to have umpired the Special Olympics youth tee ball tournament several years ago. There were so many excited kids dressed in team shirts with their gloves ready to play! One small boy who looked to be about eight or nine years old just could not hit the ball off the tee. Because the rules were very relaxed for the event, I stepped in to show him where to stand in the batter's box. At his third time batting, he had a strong look of determination on his face. By this time, he knew where to stand in the batter's box and how to stand in a batter's stance at the tee. He was ready this time! With a mighty swing, he hit the ball! It landed about six feet in front of home plate. He looked at me, and I told him to run to first base.

At that time, the pitcher, also a small boy, ran and picked up the ball and started chasing the runner. Coaches, parents, and the crowd all yelled to throw the ball, but the young pitcher continued to chase the runner around first base, almost going into the right field, but then headed toward second base, and then onward to third base. Meanwhile, everyone still yelled for the pitcher to throw the ball to one of his teammates to tag the runner out, but he still continued chasing the runner, getting close to tagging him out as they both round third. Suddenly the runner ran into one side of the third base dugout and out the other with the pitcher following behind.

The runner jumped onto home plate, and I yelled, "Safe!"

Everyone cheered and applauded while laughing. All the players came out from both dugouts and high-fived each other for the spectacular play! Now *that* is what it's all about! After the game, I gave him the ball with my signature, the date, and a message stating that he got a hit and scored.

A few years later, I saw his parents at their other child's game, where they told me that one particular game and day was so special for their son. They continued to say that he slept with the signed baseball since that game. Unfortunately, about a year after that day, he passed away. I'm humbly grateful and glad I was able to create such a lasting happy memory for that little boy and his family. It's amazing how something so simple as signing and dating a baseball can change a person's life. Every little thing you choose to say and do has an impact on someone else's life, whether you see it or not.

Jerry Blank referees an average of 30 games a week in the Memphis area — and that's not even his day job! JANUARY 1997

It always amazes me how the two worlds of baseball and basketball collide. There was a young man who came to a ball field where I was umpiring his girlfriend in softball. He looked about six feet three inches and 250 pounds and told me that when he was eight years old, his parents got a divorce. He explained that he was so angry at the time and got into trouble at school.

He mentioned that I refereed his basketball game, and at half-time, his mother asked me to talk to him, saying, "He loves you."

I remember after the game I told him, "Your game is really coming along," and he asked, "You think so?"

I replied, "Yes! Keep practicing your crossover dribbling."

Two weeks later I refereed his game again, and I noticed that his confidence and dribbling improved. Remembering my own support and influence from Coach Cordell, I told him, "To play sports, you must do well in the classroom, and then perhaps your hard work and talent could lead to a sports scholarship for college!" The now grown man told me that he just finished playing football at a large university on a scholarship, but he was most proud of being on the dean's list. He continued to say that, "Just that one little moment. That one moment in my life made a difference. Someone cared, and I never forgot that. Thanks!" I was shocked to see how I made a difference in that young man's life! You just never know on what end of a blessing you are on either the giving or the receiving end.

Another time, one grandmother told me that she just had to come to watch her grandson play basketball. She said, "All I keep hearing about is the ref!" I told her that I have more fun than the kids. Don't get me wrong, winning is great, but not at all costs.

I was refereeing a girls' sixth- and seventh-grade basketball game at Bellevue Baptist Church. I believe that I talked to the girls all through the game as usual. After the game, a lady approached me, as I noticed that everyone in the gym watched, but no one could hear what was being said. She told me, "Thank you for making this so much fun for the girls! My granddaughter was nervous, and now she cannot wait to play again!"

Later I discovered that the lady was the wife of Dr. Adrian Rogers, who was the pastor of Bellevue Baptist Church. At that time, it was a big compliment! Glad I didn't mess that up!

Some of the best times of refereeing were with flag football. There are so many youth leagues in the area! Just like basketball and baseball, I have seen so many generations of young football players come and go through the years. Again, I take the opportunities to mentor and encourage the players to be the very best they can be on the field, in the classroom, and in life.

I was out to eat with my family when a man approached my table. He was a big guy, about six feet, two inches at about 240 pounds, and asked me if I remembered him.

I replied, "Why? Do I owe you money?"

He laughed and said, "No." He continued to tell me that I officiated him playing flag football when he was seven years old.

I said, "Well, you have grown a little since then."

He explained that he now plays football for a major college team and that, thanks to me, he has learned to keep his grades up in order to keep playing. He wanted to thank me for helping him learn the game and making it fun.

It is very comforting to know that I can make a difference in someone's life just by taking the time to help them learn a sport or advising kids to stay in school. You never really know if they're listening or not at the time, but as my life has proven, they *are* listening and absorbing any wisdom you can give to help them grow and learn.

At a time, lacrosse quickly emerged and became popular in the Memphis area. The sport came onto the scene so fast there was a shortage of referees. I and a few others learned the sport and how to officiate it by calling practices before overseeing games. We did not want to make the wrong calls. You think baseball players and fans are tough? Girls in lacrosse don't play! A set of twin girls were playing on a high school team while I was refereeing. They both nearly ran me over! At first, I thought it was just one really fast player before learning that they were twins. Both were very good and talented athletes who talked to me, and I, of course, joked around with them. Toward the end of the season, they told me that I was their favorite referee and that I made the game fun for them. I told them that for my first time with lacrosse, they also made it fun for me to learn a new sport.

The parents warned me that the whole team planned to bombard me with water pistols and super soakers after the last game of the first season. I made sure I was close enough to my car before the end-of-the-game horn went off. As soon as the game ended, the girls ran to their bags to fetch the water guns and returned only to find that I was safely in my car. I laughed and yelled out of my car window, "Better luck next year!" The next year, they got me good and soaked. Some people just know how to hold a grudge.

Flag football and Lacrosse

Coaches and parents seem to play similar roles in a young person's life. Just like teachers, they help teach and lead by example and direct our youth as a positive mentor. To all of you coaches, I strongly advise to not relive your childhood or glory days through your team. Remember that it is just a game, and although it is important for the kids to learn and respect the game, in the end, it is just a game! Personally, this was and continues to be a hard lesson to witness. I have seen parents and coaches act so strict and disappointed with their children if the kids don't perform according to parent and coach expectations.

From my own relationship with my father, I know what it's like to be a child and feel like you're never going to be good enough in the eyes of your dad. To this day, I still don't believe I have ever received any true and honest praise or acknowledgment from my own father about my athletic abilities or my life successes that have made me the man that I am today. It's not a healthy way to parent and treat your children. Everyone has their own demons and personal battles to fight, and you never know just how much influence you can have on someone (good or bad) just by what you say and how you treat them. Seriously, folks, it is *just a game!* Allow your kids to grow out of self-discovery. Your job should be to help guide them and instill your wisdom to help them succeed.

I think it is so awesome to see parents and children play sports together and enjoying the game! I never had that opportunity with my father. Cherish and embrace your time together on and off the field. These are memories that last lifetimes. Time flashes by so fast, and you'll wish you spent more times in the yard playing catch or shooting hoops in the driveway or in the stands at their games. I am lucky that my youngest daughter has my athletic abilities, and she continues to play in her adult mommy life. Growing up, she played anything from soccer to basketball and softball. Although I wasn't able to step in as her official coach, I relished in the moments when I could bestow my knowledge and tips to help her develop into a strong athlete. Now I have the pleasure of umpiring her from time to time as she plays softball for our church team.

Although I missed out on bonding with my father over sports like most other kids get to do, life has come full circle and granted me the time to bond with my daughter and now my grandkids over our shared love of sports. I get to make new memories on the field with my youngest daughter as my grandkids watch us both in action, teaching them about the game. I believe this is how you leave a legacy.

While I have your attention, I would like to share a bit of wisdom: Don't yell at the umpire! Just kidding. Ha ha. (But seriously.) I talk to the parents and grandparents in the stands, getting them involved by joking around and informing them about what is going on as the game progresses. By including the crowd, I make them feel important to be there, and they are! There are several important elements to make a ball game come to life: players, coaches, officials, and the crowd. A game would be no different from a practice without the enthusiasm of the crowd cheering for their teams!

Just showing up to your child's game is a step in the right direction of showing them that you care, even if you may not understand what is going on, or you have other life obligations. Making the effort to take time every now and again to show up and support your child will speak volumes of your commitment to your family, and it will vastly strengthen your relationship and influence your child to be a better person in honoring and supporting other people in their lives. I sometimes notice kids whose parents are too busy to stay for a game and just drop them off and pick them up after the game has finished. I understand that there are other life obligations, but I have noticed some parents make a habit out of this. Your children need to be shown love through action. They need a parent, not a taxi driver. I take it upon myself to talk to those kids to let them know that they are special and important and that I'm glad they are there at the game.

One specific time I refereed back-to-back basketball games in a gym on a Saturday for several weekends. I noticed three small children, a boy about eight years old and his two sisters about six and four years old, sat together on the bleachers and stayed at that gym all day until the last game. The boy was there to play with his team in the league, but when his game ended, he sat in the bleachers, with his sisters watching the other games for the rest of the day. I noticed this happen again on the second weekend and asked them where their parents were. The boy told me that they didn't have a dad and that their mom dropped them off in the morning around 8:30 p.m. and planned to pick them up after the last game ended around 8:00 p.m.

They were well-behaved and had a few toys with them to occupy their time and snacked on a few crackers, but they were given no money to get lunch or dinner. The boy had a cell phone and said that his mom would call him when she arrived to pick them up. I didn't want to let them starve, so I bought them some candy and drinks from the concession stand.

Around lunchtime, some people went out for fast food, so I bought the kids some chicken nuggets and fries. They sat in the bleachers and had a little picnic and thanked me. I told them not to go anywhere so I could keep an eye on them. Throughout the day I kept visiting the kids to make sure they were doing well and joked around with them.

At one point the boy asked me to be his father, and I thanked him, but then told him that I'm too old to be his dad. As the last game ended for the day, I stayed with the kids until their mother finally arrived to pick them up. I walked out with the kids to meet the mom. I told her that she has such well-behaved kids, and she told me thanks and that she works a lot with no father in their lives. I informed her that the gym and the people working there are not a babysitting service and that it was upsetting that the kids were left alone for ten hours with no money to eat on. She simply dismissed this and asked how much she owed me.

I said, "Ma'am, you're missing the point. Your children need you or at least a family member who can help take care of them."

The next week, the kids were there again, but with their grand-mother and aunt. You could see the young boy light up with excite-ment as his family cheered for him and his team. The girls enjoyed their time with their grandmother and aunt learning how to and when to cheer. They just needed to be loved, supported, acknowl-edged, and cared for. Every new week the kids were joined by a new family member. One special day the kids were accompanied by about eight family members, including their mother, enjoying their time together and cheering the boy on from the bleachers! Afterward the mother gave me a hug and thanked me for helping her to swallow her pride and ask for help for the good of her children. I said that I know sometimes we get overwhelmed and life gets in the way, but the children are the priority. They all proceeded to take a family photo, and the boy took me by the hand to join them.

Sometimes I would pick a kid out who may not be the best player, the most popular, or even the brightest kid. I acknowledge them and ensure them that they are important, and then I stand back and watch the change within them as they grow and light up with encouragement! I also help other kids around to be supportive of one another. I teach them that if they're the strongest player, then protect their team, or if they're the smartest player, then help their teammates out. I help them realize that playing sports and winning games is not an individual accomplishment, but a team effort, and this lesson applies in real life too.

Chapter Nine

Can You Hold This? You're Served! Ha!

You may have heard of *Dog the Bounty Hunter*. I'm Puppy, the process server! I love my hometown of Memphis, Tennessee. I have about twelve years of experience serving legal papers in the Mid-South area, from civil warrants to subpoenas dealing with car accidents, divorces, etc. Basically, I am a glorified delivery guy for the courts. I have found that most people are basically hardworking and honest, but suffer from overextended finances, life mistakes, and some bad decisions, who just need to get out of the mess that they are in.

Aside from being a sports official, I believe I have found my calling that I was misunderstanding earlier in my life. I have the opportunity to help these people deal with the process of the court system by setting them at ease with humor and understanding. Sometimes the serves are plain and simple. Some serves are funny, some are stressful requiring quick decisions, and some are heartbreaking. The following are just a few of the many true stories that are based on actual people I have served.

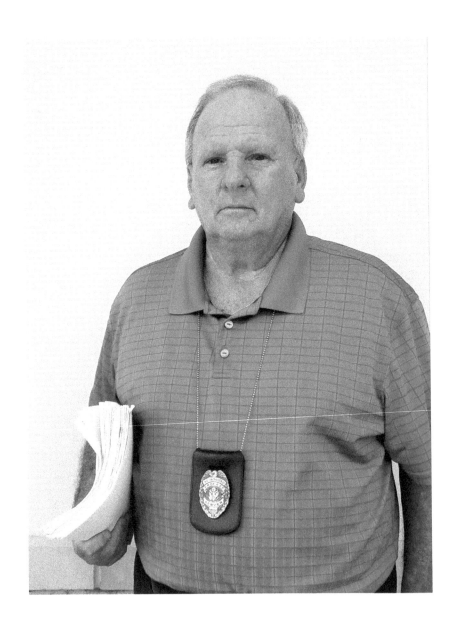

One of my very first serves involved serving divorce papers to a young lady with two small children. She opened the door, and immediately she reminded me very much of my youngest daughter, Dawn. With a heavy heart, I told her that I was sorry, but I had to give her some court papers. She said it was okay and told me that she had been expecting them. She noticed how upset I was and kept reassuring me that it was all okay. The next day, she even called the office to see if I was doing well since it seemed to have bothered me more than it did her, which made my boss laugh. I just found the whole situation very sad, thinking about how similar the young woman was to my own daughter.

I had to serve an order of protection to a thirty-year-old male in Mississippi. Two of his neighbors filed for an order of protection because he threatened them. One neighbor had a party, of which some of their guests parked in front of the defendant's house. The defendant got mad and went toward the house and threatened the neighbor as well as the guests. He told them to move their vehicles, or he was going to start breaking windows and slashing tires. That was when the two neighbors decided to file for the order of protection.

One weekday morning around 6:00 a.m., I was at the defendant's address to serve him. As I drove up to the house, I noticed it was a mobile home with a huge wood deck on the front, about five feet off the ground, flanked by two staircases on either side. Right after getting out of my car, I noticed two large dogs chained to both staircases, leaving no pathway to the front door.

I called out, yelling, "Hello?"

No answer was received, and I then honked my horn several times. Finally, a male about five feet nine inches and about 180 pounds came storming out of the door to the end of the deck and asked, "What the F*@k do you want?"

I asked him what his name was, and he told me, which matched the name on the document. I met him at the deck's edge, where he bent over to see the paper as I informed him about it. I asked him to sign it to prove that I served him personally. He took my offered ink pen and the paper from me, stormed to the front door, and then turned around and threw my pen at me.

I said, "That's okay. You're served!"

The defendant got mad and said, "I'm going to kick your ass!"

At that point, a female poked her out of the front door and asked what was going on. The guy told her to get back into the house, to which she shut the door. The guy then turned toward me and began to charge, diving like Superman. off the deck at me. I simply sidestepped, and he hit the ground hard, making a loud thud, knocking the breath out of him. I guess he forgot that the deck was high off the ground.

I said, "What's wrong with you? Are you crazy?"

He couldn't answer, but just stared at me. I heard a neighbor's voice from across the street reply, "Yes he is!"

That neighbor informed me that the defendant does have some mental issues and is required to be on medication, even though he had not taken them lately. With the guy still on the ground, the neighbor proceeded to tell me that he was a nice guy if he stayed on his medication.

We both asked him if he was okay, and he replied, "Yes, but I think I sprained my shoulder."

Once he calmed down due to his injury, I served him the paper and showed him his court date and the phone numbers to call if he had questions. We all shook hands and called it a day.

Sometimes I have defendants that avoid the process of service. In these cases, I leave a written notice that explains the repercussions of avoiding the process of service, providing a phone number to reach me as soon as they can. If I have their phone number, I will call and more than likely end up leaving a voice mail. If I am so lucky to reach them on the phone, they won't always agree on a time and place to meet me to complete the service.

This example happened with an elected Memphis city official. He did not return my several voice mails and written notices that I left with family members at his home. I went to his office to serve the papers to him personally. I made two attempts and was told that he was not available or not in the office. I asked his assistant to call him, to which I was told they also got his voice mail and left a message. I even left a written notice with the office personnel and instructed him to have the defendant call me. I finally got a tip that he would be in his office one afternoon during the week.

On a weekday in downtown Memphis, I arrived at the office around 1:00 p.m. I saw the defendant in the back hallway of the office, and he spotted me. He then took off and got on the elevator at the back of the office. The receptionist tried to call him on his phone and told me he just left. I went down the stairs to look for him coming out of the building. I saw him several yards away getting onto a trolley car, thinking I couldn't catch him. At that time, a carriage used for tourists to sightsee the downtown area came by. I stopped the carriage driver and asked him to follow the trolley.

Seeing my badge, the driver asked, "Are we in pursuit?"

I told him to just relax and get me close to the trolley. After about ten minutes, we caught up to the trolley that was stopped by a red light. From there, I boarded the trolley and instructed the driver to hold on for a minute as I walked to the back where I served the defendant.

The elected official said, "I can't believe you came after me!"

I replied that he should've called me, and we could've avoided all this drama. After the serve, I got back into the carriage and rode back to my car, asking the driver how much I owed.

He replied, "Nothing. That's the most excitement I've had in a month!"

I thanked him with a tip and suggested that he get out more often. In this line of work, you just never know what will happen. Although I could have let the defendant leave, I was determined to complete that serve. It became a challenge I couldn't refuse. Like all other moments in my life, I think that the carriage was sent to me at just the right moment to help me complete the serve. The driver didn't have to give me a free ride, which goes to show that everyone can make the choice to help others in need, and others have a choice to make life more difficult, like the elected official.

There was a lady who also tried to evade service when I tried to serve a subpoena to her because she was a witness to a crime, but she was scared to come forward. I tried on several different occasions to meet with her, but she was never home or never showed up to meet.

I was able to catch her husband at home, and he mentioned that she travels out of town a lot for her job.

One fateful day, I was tipped that the lady was at home. Thinking on my feet to ensure she wouldn't evade me again, I stopped by a pizza place and got an empty pizza box while on the way to her house. I pulled up to the house, acting like a disheveled, older, hippie pizza guy with my music blaring loudly in the car, my shirt untucked and unbuttoned, and sunglasses on. The husband answered the door, but thanks to our first meeting being about two weeks ago and my sunglasses, he didn't recognize me.

I said, "Jones?"

The husband said, "Nope. Wrong house!"

I replied, "Man! This is the second time this has happened to me today!"

I began to walk away but then stopped and said, "I can't return this back to the store. Do you want a free pizza?"

A female voice from behind the door asked what kind it was. Suddenly the lady I had been trying to serve appeared at the door to check out the free pizza. I opened the pizza box, revealing the subpoena inside!

I simply stated, "You have been served," and told them to call the attorney to get the issue taken care of.

She said, "Man, you are good!"

I said, "Yes, I am!"

In most cases, people expect the court papers, but in others, I am an unwelcome surprise delivering bad news. One beautiful Saturday afternoon around 12:30 p.m. I was making one last stop to serve my last paper of the day at a house in a nice residential neighborhood before going home. The papers were just hospital bills. I visited this residence several times before, but with no luck in catching someone at home or having anyone contact me from the notice cards that I left. This particular day I knocked on the door several times with no answer, but as I turned to walk back to my car parked on the street, I heard a loud thud.

A man came charging out of the house, yelling, "Who's knocking on my door?"

Showing my badge, I said his name, to which he confirmed while raising and pointing a handgun at me. I started to slowly back down his driveway with my hands up, explaining who I was and why I was there. He started moving toward me, still pointing the gun and aiming at my head.

I could see him get emotional with anger, fighting back tears, saying, "I should just kill you!"

I replied, "Don't do it. Just put the gun down."

As the man continued to follow me down his driveway, I noticed that he saw something over my left shoulder. I was too afraid to look and turn my back on him.

The man suddenly began to lower his gun, and told me, "This is your lucky day," and went back into his house.

I definitely, without a doubt, had an angel looking out for me at that moment. Sure enough, I turned around to find that angel across the street. A neighbor witnessed the entire scene while washing his car in his driveway.

I crossed the street to him and said, "I think you just saved my life," and then I called the police.

The police came and arrested the guy, while I and the neighbor filled out reports. A few weeks later, I was summoned to the district attorney's office, where I learned that they wanted to take the case to criminal court, causing the guy to serve time in jail if I were to press charges. I was able to read the paperwork about the details of the case, and I learned that the guy had a legal permit for his handgun; he had never been in trouble, with no track record, and maintained a great job.

His pastor and employer were there, vouching for his clean record. It turns out that his wife just went through surgery due to a life-threatening illness, which was what the hospital bills were for that I tried to serve. I apparently was the last straw that made him snap under all the pressure. I was able to see the guy again, and I told him that I respected his right to carry the gun, but he must be able to carry responsibly, not letting his emotions pull the trigger. I declined to press charges against him, but he ended up getting a long probation and was enrolled into anger management, along with the law requiring him to reapply for his handgun permit. He thanked me for showing mercy.

Reflecting on that day, I really thought it was going to be my last day, so I asked the guy if he was really going to shoot me. He thought for a moment and said that he really didn't know. Since that incident, we have crossed paths several times through the years, and he went out of his way to shake my hand with a hug, always thanking me for giving him a second chance. I believe I was his angel that day, to have changed his perspective on life and on carrying a gun by showing compassion and love in such an emotionally heightened situation.

Among serving papers, I also oversee writ of possessions, also known as evictions, setting people and their belongings out on the curb due to unpaid rent. Most of them that I do, the tenants have already vacated the premises. In some cases, people only pay one month of rent the whole time living in an apartment, house, or another rental property, forcing the landlord to spend three months evicting them to reclaim the property. Some people work the system by filing bankruptcy or lie about being served or being warned about the eviction. Some people don't care about their own property or anyone else's.

One winter morning around 9:00 a.m. I arrived at a small older single-family home. I had a locksmith join me to change the locks for the landlord and two laborers to move the tenants' belongings out of the house. I knocked on the door and identified myself as an officer of the courts. At that time a small, older model car drove up. A female in her late twenties got out, leaving the male driver inside. She asked what we were doing, to which I informed her, and she replied that her grandmother was inside the house, bedridden on dialysis, and that she was calling the police.

I said, "Okay. We will wait."

After a while, two officers arrived, and I showed them the writ of possession paper. The officers then showed the paper to the lady, explaining to her that my crew and I were correct to proceed with our job.

I entered the house for a quick walk-through, looking for a grandmother, but found nobody. The officers were still there as I came back outside.

I told the lady, "You need to make a report with the officers because someone has stolen your grandmother!"

She obviously didn't think that was too funny and drove off. The officers asked if everything was all right, and I said yes, and so they left.

As a protocol on a writ of possession, I entered the house again to check all drawers, cabinets, and closets to see if there might be hidden weapons, money, or drugs. The house was older and extremely hot from leaving the heat on high coming through the floor furnaces. I opened the back door to let some of the heat out. I walked to the last bedroom, and I noticed there was an undiscovered closet around the corner with a steel knife stuck in the molding, locking the door. In the past, when I saw this, there were dogs stuck in the closets. So I carefully removed the knife, but I was not prepared for what I found.

When I opened the door, I saw a young boy about seven years old, lying on a blanket inside. I almost lost it, as this moment brought me back to my own childhood, being thrown and locked inside a closet for who knows how long. Luckily, this kid's mom didn't try to burn the house down, although it might have happened by how hot the floor furnaces were that day. The young boy wore what looked like a school uniform—consisting of a white polo and khaki pants. As the light from outside hit his face, he covered his eyes with his hands.

He said, "Please don't hurt me, mister."

I showed him my badge and said, "Son, I'm not here to hurt you. I'm here to help you."

He came out of the closet, and I could see that he had been in there for quite some time, since he stained his pants. What I remember most was his big smile and the tight hug he gave me. I asked who put him there, and he told me it was his mother. I asked how long he was in there, and he asked what day it was. I told him it was Monday, and he said he was in there since Saturday night.

As I escorted him outside, the lady and guy drove up again. The lady told the boy to come on. He jumped off the porch, got in the car, and they drove off. Before they got too far, I got the plate number and called the police to let them know of the situation. One officer that had previously been there returned, and I explained to him what happened as my crew finished the job. The officer informed me that they stopped the car, where they discovered that the male driver had no license, no insurance, and had an outstanding warrant. They also found that the lady was on probation for child neglect, and the both of them were arrested with possession of drugs and paraphernalia. The young boy was taken to his grandmother's house.

About a month after this incident, I was at the courts, where I ran into the young boy and his grandmother who was there to get full custody.

He had the same big smile and told his grandmother, "Grandmama, that's the man that saved me."

Holding back my tears, I talked to him, telling him to mind his grandmother, to help her out, and most importantly, to go to school and do his homework.

I told him, "I gave your grandmother my phone number, so don't give her any trouble. She loves you."

I found out that he likes basketball. Since I'm a referee, I was able to get him into an afterschool program, and I explained to him that he needed to keep his grades up in order to play.

I left, telling him, "I'll see you on the basketball court and not the courthouse!"

That encounter helped me feel better about having to deal with all the negativity that comes with doing my job. It's a great comfort to know that sometimes things *do* turn out well for some of the people who are involved in these situations.

Chapter Ten

Ha!

I believe that people and moments are meant to come into our lives to either teach us a lesson, influence us for the better, or challenge us. Some people are meant to simply pass through our lives, leaving a lasting impression on us, and some are meant to stay and become a part of our life. I try to be a considerate person, aware of others by simply saying hello and acknowledging them. In today's world, people get so caught up within themselves that society lacks the simple and effective face-to-face, in-person connection.

Humor keeps me going and helps me to overcome the trials and tribulations of life. I believe that helping others can be therapeutic for the soul. Making people laugh is a gift that I love to share, which helps make little improvements in the world, like brightening up someone's day and making new friends. Throughout my whole life, there have been many comedians who have greatly influenced my humor: Red Skelton, Lucille Ball, Carol Burnett, Tim Conway, The Three Stooges, Steve Martin, Jim Belushi, Chevy Chase, John Candy, Chris Farley, Jim Carrey, Adam Sandler, and Robin Williams. However, Jerry Lewis is the main comedian who has had a major impact on my life and humor, with his impeccable physical comedy, timing, and his quick wit to improvise in any given situation. Learning from Jerry Lewis, I practice and apply my simple dad jokes and practical jokes in real life, giving a small gift of spontaneity and joy to break down walls that we all put up as we go through the monotonous routines of life.

I don't think we just happen to meet people along our life journey just by chance. We only have a small window to say or do something positive to encourage others to think differently or sometimes just to think. One day while working, I got into an elevator with six other people. Four were female, and two were male; and all six of them were texting on their cell phones, not saying a word and not even looking up from their devices to acknowledge anyone else who was crammed in beside them. Well, of course, I couldn't stand the silence and seized the opportunity with a captivated audience, so I requested that one of the ladies press the button for the twelfth floor. I watched as she searched each and every row of buttons only to find out that there was no twelfth-floor button. Everyone stopped to witness the joke, and we all laughed. I said, "See, we all needed a laugh today!" and they all agreed.

I find that a lot of people are going through life just trying to survive the day, who may need encouragement with a side of laughter to make their day a great one! One day I was out to lunch with my oldest daughter, Michelle, in a popular restaurant located in downtown Memphis that is always busy for lunch rushes. After we finally were seated, our flustered and exhausted waitress greeted us for our drink orders. She seemed to be very stressed from running around, so I decided to give her a laugh.

As we placed our orders, I asked for the "Honeymoon salad."

With a puzzled look on her face, she asked, "What is that?"

I told her, "Lettuce alone."

She paused and thought for a moment, and then I could see the light bulb go on! She laughed out loud so hard that everyone in the restaurant turned to see what happened. The waitress told me that I was funny and thanked me for making her laugh, continuing to say that she needed it that particular day. After that day, I get into the restaurant right away if that waitress was working.

I believe laughter changes everything, making people smile and forget their troubles and worries even for just a moment in the day. However, telling jokes off the cuff to random strangers and family and friends is one thing, but getting on a stage with a micro-phone, a spotlight in your face, and club owners telling me to be funny is a completely different ball game, making it a formality and nerve-racking.

When I was sixty-three, my son told me about a local bar that he and his friends went to for karaoke learning that they also had an open-mic night for comedians. My son said that they stayed to watch some comedians, only to find out that one was funny, but most of them were just outright vulgar.

He told me, "Dad, you're funnier than most of those people I saw, and your material is clean! You should try doing stand-up comedy!"

My son was not the first person to try to coax me to do stand-up comedy. I have had a longtime friend who actually owns a local comedy club, and he has been telling me to get on the stage and try out my jokes. All I had were dad jokes and one-liners, and all of a sudden, I had to write and organize a set to perform on stage in front of professional and local comedians! My son has experience with performing on stage, and he has a degree in acting, so he instantly began to apply his wisdom to help me rehearse and organize my jokes to tell a story and, most importantly, to not be awkward on stage.

To familiarize myself with this new world of comedy, my family joined me to just go watch the open-mic night to learn. I was surprised to see that most of the jokes were nasty and off-color. One young man just talked about how many times he had sex, but after chatting with him, I realized that his stories of sex were more than likely self-inflicted. *Ha!* The female comedians were not any better and sometimes even more vulgar than the guys! I personally don't think that you have to be nasty and vulgar in order to be funny.

The next week, I went to try out my material (I do write my own stuff). There was about six of us, and the crowd was a decent size, and my wife and son were there for support. I ended up going last. As the MC called me up, my owner friend told me to just do my thing and be myself. Most of the other comedians were young, and there I was, an older white guy at a hip-hop comedy club, not sure if I would get some laughs or be booed off the stage. I got up on stage and ran through my performance. I was supposed to only go for ten minutes, but I ended up going for about twenty-five minutes. To my surprise and relief, everyone laughed! Later I told my wife that I never had to wait for people to stop laughing before telling another joke! I felt accepted! The other comics gave me high fives, and the owner and his son asked me to come back!

People approached my wife, saying they appreciated that my jokes were clean and that it was a breath of fresh air from what most of the other comics do. People told me I was funny and to keep it up! So I reconvened with my comedy crew, my wife and son, and we began to work on creating more setlists and planning other stand-up ideas for future performances. Whenever my family and I went out to eat, we jotted down jokes and funny situations on napkins and little sheets of paper after trying out my comedy on the waitstaff. After a while, my wife finally started carrying around a little notepad to save her purse from the thousands of written-on napkins. I frequented the comedy club several times, trying out new material and adjusting my sets accordingly.

There was a night where the club had a comedy competition that I entered! There were nineteen contestants with several from out of town. The club was packed, and the contest started at 8:00 p.m., and I didn't go on until three hours later. I had a great set, holding my own against some seasoned veterans.

As I exited the stage, handing the mic back to the MC, he said, "That was the cleanest set I have ever heard. You didn't say one curse word, did you?"

I replied, "Hell no!" causing him to do a double take and laugh.

A guy from Florida ended up winning, but later the club owner told me that I almost won and that I was the funniest from the local Memphis area. From that point on, I started going to other clubs around the area about three times a week for several months.

There was another club that I decided to try. It was a gay and lesbian bar with a smaller crowd. I had to enter the stage through a door from behind while walking through a silver tensile curtain. As

I came onstage, everyone stopped talking and stared in confusion, seeing an older white guy out of place in a gay bar.

I said, "You didn't know you were going to get this tonight, did you? Coming through that backstage door, I felt like I just literally came out of the closet!"

They all laughed, cutting the tension, realizing that I'm not who I appear to be. I could tell that most of them labeled me as an old-school, Bible-thumping, hard-core Republican, who did not belong in a gay bar. Later my son said that he knew they were either going to love you or hate you, to which I replied, "Such is life!"

At another local club was a large, mixed crowd of young, old, and several different sexes. Again I was well received! Most of the other comics were college age to young-adult age, mainly talking about politics and legalizing marijuana, but there I was again, keeping it clean and making several generations of different backgrounds unite in laughter. The one thing that I have learned is, how you go about treating people does matter. Everyone matters in this world. People were high-fiving me, saying that I made them laugh, and I even gained a new fan who happened to be a drag queen. Throughout the next year, I continued to visit several other clubs from country western bars, gay bars, hip-hop bars, and even an Elvis-themed restaurant, practicing my skills; and I never once strayed from my clean comedy. However, with my job requiring my days to start at 4:00 a.m. and with my age, I had to slow down.

After a while of not doing stand-up, a nationally televised talent competition was having open-call auditions locally. I sent a video of my talent. They called me, and the representative told me that she personally saw my video and thought I was very funny. She asked me if I was planning on attending the auditions in person.

Of course, I said, "Yes. I will be there."

The day of the auditions, I went alone and stood in a very long line at 8:00 a.m. Two official-looking people filtered through the line, asking for participants' names. They got to me and told me to go with them. As we passed all the people in line, I got strange and confused looks from auditionees, wondering who I was and why I was getting "special treatment" to hop to the front. Once I reached the front of the line, I met a lady who gave me my audition packet. As she pulled up my information on her computer, I saw the words "see video."

While standing there, she proceeded to watch my audition video and said, "Yes, it was great. We're happy that you are here. Good luck!"

While waiting in the talent holding area, I met many different people from all over the country. I told jokes and socialized with hundreds of auditionees, helping to calm them down and forget their nervousness for a few moments. We were assigned a number and waited to be called into groups for the first round of auditions. If you missed your called number, you lost the opportunity to audition.

About five hours later, my number was finally called to join my group and go into the first round of auditions. My group consisted of fifteen auditionees, ranging from several singers, dancers, a juggler, a whistler, and one other comedian along with myself. The first round was judged by three people, who gave each act ten minutes to show their talent. I nervously watched as people in my group were randomly called one by one to perform in front everyone and the judges.

Each act dropped like flies, unsuccessfully executing their talents. I was called last out of my whole group. Once the judges realized that I was doing comedy, they expressed that they hoped I was a clean act since they just sent two comics away for being too vulgar. I assured them that I was clean, saying I just showered that morning. I started with my first joke, making my entire group *and* all three judges laugh. I had to tell everyone to stop laughing and wait until the end since I only had ten minutes, and of course, they all laughed at that comment!

After my group finished, the judges asked everyone to leave except for me. After the room cleared, leaving me alone with the three judges, they proceeded to thank me for being a "breathe of fresh air" with a "very clean and very funny" act. They asked me many questions to learn more about me, and they even asked where I got most of my material, learning that I write most of my own stuff.

Next, they all told me to follow them into another audition room, where there were four more judges. They asked me to do my routine again for the new judges, informing me that this was considered my "round 2" audition. I did so, but I took a chance and added more material since I had more time with a captive audience of seven judges. One of my jokes was about a treadmill causing two of the judges to laugh hysterically as one gave me the okay sign with her hand.

Several jokes later, everyone laughed, and I felt like I was on a good roll! One lady from the first set of judges informed the others that I added new material in the short amount of time since the first round! Each one of the seven judges provided feedback, and they all agreed that I was very naturally funny, but I needed some polishing. They then informed me that I would hear something in about two weeks, so I thanked them for their time and feedback. Two weeks later, I received a phone call where I was told that I did well and impressed the judges and that I was very close to making the cut, but I needed more experience and stage time to polish my craft.

The whole audition was a great learning experience and was very encouraging for me to become more confident in my talent. I am appreciative for going as far into the audition process as I did with having but a few amateur performances under my belt. I'm still planning to continue my comedy as well as continue to be my same old goofy self who interacts with strangers just to keep spreading the laughter and joy of life!

Chapter Eleven

Sometimes Our Life's Purpose Is to Serve as a Warning to Others. Ha!

Now at the ripe old age of sixty-five after living through a total knee replacement and a double bypass heart surgery, I'm finding out that aging sucks! I now have knee troubles and need glasses to read, and my "get up and go" has "got up and went." Ha! I may be sixty-five, but I read at a sixty-six level. However, even at my age, there are a lot of sixty-five-year-olds who are not as agile and energetic as I still am.

My whole life I have always given my best effort, and I still continue to strive to live my best day every day to the best that I can with passion, drive, and compassion, with the help of family, friends, coworkers, and grandchildren. My life has been a series of twists and turns and ups and downs, but I wouldn't change it at all. It has shaped me into the person that I am today. I'm not a scientist, and I cannot prove how important human interaction can be to affecting a person's life for good or bad. I choose to continue to send laughter and love into the world in hopes that it will inspire others to pay it forward, creating a ripple effect of good deeds, making the world a happier place. From my sixty-five years (and counting) of life experiences, I can honestly say that it does not hurt to help motivate and be positive for others to make people feel loved through acknowledgment and respect.

There was a moment when I was in an office building that I often visit for work, standing in the lobby, chatting with a friend. At that time a large, well-dressed man walked by us as our eyes met. I noticed he was not in the best of moods at that moment from the huge frown on his face.

I said, "It's a great day!"

He replied, "For you maybe," as he passed on by.

I then countered, "It can be for you also! Make it a great one!"

The large man stopped, turned, and looked at me.

I continued, "Make today great! We only have one today! Not everyone has a tomorrow."

He just simply turned and walked out the door without a word. A few moments later, I was still chatting with my friend in the lobby when the large man returned. I surely thought I was going to get beat up at this moment. He walked up to me and shook my hand. He apologized for being rude to me and explained that I made him stop to think about what I said.

He proceeded to hug me, saying, "God sent you to me, didn't He?"

I said, "Yes, He did!"

Suddenly this large man began to cry. He told me that he received bad news the day before from his doctor. I asked him to pray with me, and we did. He mentioned that he was a Christian, but he wasn't doing much for God as a Christian should.

I told him, "Today is your great day!"

He agreed and said, "Yes, it is!"

I said, "Now go help someone else!"

It just goes to show that if you take the time to observe and acknowledge others in this world, you can make a much-needed impact on a person's life. I speak to most everyone who crosses my path, saying "Hello, have a good day!" or open a door for them, saying, "Thank you," and "You're welcome." Sometimes people will give me a strange look, some people don't say a thing or even make eye contact with me; but for the most part, I can see a physical change in people as they begin to smile and come alive with joy. I can only hope that my little interactions help add to their day for the better.

You too have the ability to make small changes in the world for the better through small acts of kindness. Integrity is an important quality to have to do the right thing when no one else is looking; however, some people try to do the right thing for all the wrong reasons. The point is that we need to take responsibility for our actions and maintain our own integrity for ourselves and our character, as well as our community.

I once stood in a fast-food line, and I wanted to test this theory of people's integrity. I purposely dropped a ten dollar bill on the floor to see if anyone would pick it up and keep it or give it back to me. Nine out of ten people returned the money. One person looked around to see if anyone else noticed the money on the ground before grabbing it and leaving. What would you do in that scenario?

As simple as it may seem, it is a true test of someone's character, don't you think? It is easy to get mad at that dishonest person, but if you have an open mind and broaden your view, you may see a different side from that person's perspective. Everyone lives life at different stages and, therefore, has different experiences of growth in his or her own time. Perhaps that person really needed ten dollars at that moment in their life? If not, I believe that dishonesty will see justice at some point in one way or another.

My occupations of process serving and umpire/refereeing may not be universally ideal, but I get to meet so many different people from different backgrounds, ages, cultures, and locations. I have seen that most people are good. There is only a very small percentage of people in the world that are bad and evil, who seem to always be in the spotlight. You know you have seen and met them. However, I truly believe that most people in the world are just good, wholesome, hardworking people trying to find their own piece of happiness in life.

My piece of advice as to one of the many secrets of life is to find what you are called to do in this life. Find what makes you special and what you love to do and then use it to the best of your abilities with passion and compassion to make the world a better place. I believe we are not born by accident, but rather born with a purpose. Find out why you are here. Don't just go through life without actually living it! Get out of your own way, broaden your perspective and your soul, then stand back and see how God can bless your life.

Sometimes we need to ask for forgiveness, sometimes we need to give forgiveness to others, and sometimes we need to forgive others for ourselves to move on with our own lives. It's okay to remember the past, but we don't need to live in it. The past is your past, and it is where you came from. You can't change that, but you can change your future. Remember and learn from your past to inform your future. Remember those who helped mold you into the person you are or the person you want to become and then be that better person for others in your future. Happiness comes from what you do, how you do it, and whom you choose to share it with. Affect the world in a positive way and leave the world a better place than when you came into it.

I don't intend to come off preachy, but I want to express the importance of everyone and their existence in this life. I have witnessed so many people just going through the motions of life, forgetting to enjoy all the joys of life! I also have learned about several friends and acquaintances who have committed suicide out of depression and hopelessness. This should not happen. Life is way too precious to give up no matter what the difficulties are. There is a plan for everyone's life, and with God and His angels, you are never hopeless or alone. We have the choice to make the change to live for today and bloom where we are.

I know that every one of us is fighting our own personal battles behind closed doors and inside our own minds, just trying to survive. It is a fight worth fighting to not give up or give in to temptations, letting evil destroy your life through financial problems, divorce, drugs, alcohol, etc. Staying positive and motivated is no easy task, but the reward of happiness is worth it, and it all starts with you! Tomorrow is never a guarantee. Now is the time. Now is your time!

Laugh and find the joy in your life that gives you reason and purpose to live. I believe that humor can be a universal language to help bridge our many differences. I believe that humor is one of life's best medicines. Jokes and funny situations help us through the mundane routines of life and make us aware and present to laugh and enjoy life.

Writing this book has surprisingly been therapeutic, and in turn, it has helped my siblings begin to heal in dealing with and revisiting the dark issues from our past. Hopefully, this book has made you laugh and inspired you to appreciate life, yourself, and others in your life and in this world. Kindness along with humor and laughter are all common languages to reach others and unite our differences, as well as help console and heal. Life is not a race; it's a journey, and even now at the age of sixty-five, I continue on with my journey through life with love, passion, compassion, and laughter, awaiting new experiences, whatever they may be. Remember…

Sometimes you just gotta laugh!

COVER ART STORY

My son, Jason, has a talent for graphic arts. He specializes in photo manipulations, ensuring to always tell a story in each design he creates. Through our collaboration process, he designed the artwork for this book cover after I shared a story I once heard several years ago that I kept near and dear to my heart. This set up the inspiration for me to begin writing this book in hopes to share my wisdom and encourage others who may be in need.

The Story

One hot summer, a pastor was on vacation with his family in the desert, touring an old, western ghost town. The place was very aged with time and desolate with the occasional tumbleweed passing by. As he walked down Main Street, he noticed a dirt road off to the side, littered with trash and dead weeds. Among all the dirt, trash, and dead plants, the hot sun shined a beam of light, highlighting a bright-red rose that stood in full bloom right in the middle of the alleyway. The pastor interpreted this picture as a symbol of life, meaning that anyone can make their life better and be happy no matter what background they came from.

The Design

This story is the perfect symbolism for my entire life and this book! However, Jason and I wanted to modify the pastor's vision into a more updated scene representative of today's fast-paced world. Among the hustle and bustle of daily life, people, especially children, can become forgotten, cast aside, and lost. A dark, urban alleyway provides the appropriate environment for such a theme evoking a feeling of a scary, dark, and lonely place similar to the ghost town. The cracked pavement signifies the pain and scars from the hardships of life, and the puddles suggest tears shed by a suffering soul. Instead of using a rose, which inevitably means romance and love, Jason and I discussed other possible symbolic flowers. Through research, we discovered that the blue iris represents faith and hope, representing the sole message and purpose of this book. Additionally, Jason included a ray of heavenly light illuminating the symbol of hope to show that no matter where you live and no matter what your circumstances are, there is always hope even in the darkest of places.

About the Author

Jerry L. Blank is faith, family, and funny. Born and raised and still residing in Memphis, Tennessee, Jerry interacts with several different people in his day-to-day life through work, sports, church, and recreation. He balances the heavy-hearted job of legal process serving with the pleasures of umpiring and refereeing ball games. When he's not in the courts or on the ball fields, he dabbles in stand-up comedy. Despite his upbringing, Jerry always had a natural talent in finding the humor out of life even in the darkest of moments. He credits his hidden love and talent for writing to his mother, Lila, who always wrote letters, notes, and cards. Jerry has written several fictional works that have gone unpublished, but *Bloom Where You Are* is a personal and therapeutic labor of inspiration, humor, and love.

CPSIA information can be obtained
at www.ICGtesting.com
Printed in the USA
BVHW060823240619
551798BV00015B/551/P